MACCLESFIELD MAN

The memoirs of a pig-headed Maxonian

Raymond Maddock

ACKNOWLEDGMENTS

My thanks must go to my niece, Susan Gater for her assistance with proof reading and checking the grammar of my book prior to publication.
I am also indebted to Brian Ollier photographic studio for the scanning of the pictures and the design of the front cover.

ALSO BY THE SAME AUTHOR

MACCLESFIELD DEMOLISHED BUT NOT FORGOTTEN
ANSON GAS AND OIL MUSEUM 2005

Front cover of the book: Easter camp Wincle 1957

CHURNET VALLEY BOOKS
1 King Street, Leek, Staffordshire. 01538 399033
www.leekbooks.co.uk

ISBN 1 904546 38 2

CONTENTS

MECCA

My bedroom over the shop at 20 Cross Street in the building to the left of the picture.

My picture taken in July 1948 at the age of eleven.

IN THE BEGINNING

I was born on the 4th May 1937 at number 9 Cedar Grove, Heaton Moor, in Stockport, the first child of Mr Leonard Leoville Ponting and Alice Ponting formally Alice Constance Maddock. My father already had two girls from his previous wife, Lola Elizabeth and Rose Winder who became my half sisters. There was later a younger sister Rene Winifred and a brother Kenneth which completed my immediate family, although my father went on to have other offspring by other women.

Heaton Moor was a district of Stockport which was, when I was born part of Cheshire, although it later became part of Manchester under the boundary changes. I left my home in Stockport when I was still a baby to live in Rainow, opposite the Church, so I feel I can be justified in calling myself a Macclesfield Man.

My mother's parents did not approve of my father and I have no evidence that they were ever actually married. I understand that she first met him in Congleton where she worked at Conlowes employed as a baby sitter to my half sisters. She must have loved him as she defied her parents and took on his two young children when their own mother deserted them. I am sure my grandparents were right - in my opinion my father was not a good man. Amongst other things he served a prison sentence for the theft of lead from the roof of Trinity Church in Cumberland Street.

I have no recollection of my home in Rainow but my half-sister Rose tells me that I would sit outside in my pram and watch the buses go by. The family did not stay there long and soon we moved into rented accommodation at number 157 Chester Road, Macclesfield. This was a large four storey house which was also 155 the home of a Mr and Mrs Dakin who were in the decorating trade. Our part of the building was accessed down a short drive to the rear of number 155 and overlooked the fields of the neighbouring farmer, Mr Brocklehurst.

The house has long since been demolished and replaced by a large block of flats which do not rival the old house at all in appearance. The field is now the site of Macclesfield's fire and ambulance station. What remained of the farm would later be the new T/A barracks, when the Cheshire Regiment moved from the Drill Hall in Bridge Street, and the All Hallow's playing fields.

We kept ducks and chickens in our large garden to the rear of the house and my sister Rene got pleasure out of picking up the ducks by their beaks and swinging them round. I doubt the ducks enjoyed it but I suspect my sister thought that they did. My eldest sister used to pick up worms and she would draw them between her lips which I found very alarming. I think that is why she did it but it put me off worms for life even though I have no dread of other creepy crawlies.

On one occasion I was climbing on the fence at the bottom of our garden which overlooked a small stream, when one of my very new sandals came off and I watched it roll down the steep bank into the water and float away, never to be seen again. Needless to say I was not very popular with my mother for that.

We like many others had an underground air raid shelter which was never used as far as I am aware but it was a great place to play or hide. I had a little red peddle car in which my younger sister and I spent many happy hours going up and down our front drive. The only holiday I had with my mother was two days in New Brighton where I enjoyed boating on the small lake and a paddle in the sea.

When I was only a few months old I had intersusception which is an interlocking of the intestine. Another time I landed in the isolation hospital on Moss Lane, now the Weston nursing home, with scarlet fever and pneumonia. I did of course, like all the kids, go through the mumps and measles season, no big deal in those days - kids today are just too clean and healthy for their own good. The only other thing we all suffered from on occasions was the dreaded nits, soon dealt with by the nit nurse. We did also go to the clinic in Pierce Street for a dental examination although during wartime sweets were in short supply so decay was not a problem.

EARLY DAYS, EXTRACT OF AN ARTICLE IN THE MACCLESFIELD EXPRESS

My earliest memory was of our front door bell ringing without anyone having turned the handle outside. I was later to discover that this was caused by German flying bombs passing over our house. One landed behind the Blacksmiths Arms at Henbury and one on Acton Farm, Over Alderley.

My second most vivid memory was of being scolded by our next door neighbour, Mrs Dakin from 155. It was obviously my earliest attempt to be self-employed, as I had removed all the blooms from Mrs Dakin's lilac bush and assembled them in several large jam jars inside our air raid shelter. I had somehow planned to take the blooms to market.

My first morning at Athey Street school passed off well apart from the fact that when we were let out at playtime I walked home thinking it was the end of the school day and my mother had to take me back. My journey to and from school, undertaken on my own after the first few days, was very interesting as I had to pass the home of our headmistress, Miss Sheldon, on Chester Road. Directly opposite her house was a large house now used as a prep school but then occupied by the Americans. I always stopped to stare as on the front lawn grazed a small pony. The pony would frequently walk calmly past the sentry, out onto the road and down to the farm where it spent some time making friends with Mr Brocklehurst's horse who pulled the milk float. As there was no traffic on Chester Road in those days the pony seemed to commute at will. Although I loved to see the pony I was a little scared of it - I would always go behind the gate and peep at it from a safe vantage point.

The rest of my journey to school took me down Clowes Street and past the card

factory, where on my way home they would give me off cuts of cardboard. I thought it a wonderful gift, only given to me. After crossing Oxford Road I went along Cottage Street where the old cinder playing field was covered with the tents of more American forces with many large lorries and guns. The sentry on the gate was always very friendly and would offer us chewing gum and a friendly smile.

I always did well at Athey Street and I was successful in passing my eleven plus. I was given a place at the Kings School but there I was not so clever.

I will not forget the winter of '47 when the snow was above my head on the journey to school. On arrival we all had to sit in the hall until Miss Sheldon told us that the boiler had burst and we all had to go home as there was no heating in the school. An unexpected holiday and snow as well.

The most important effect on my life whilst attending Athey Street, was Mrs Wardle who, if we were good, would read us a chapter from Wind in the Willows by Kenneth Graham. This book gave me an early desire to study natural history and become a part of the living world, not just another exploiter of the planet.

To get back to my story, I remember the day I saw my first black man. I was in Chester Road when I saw this huge American in uniform across the road. I was so astonished because I thought all black men were in Africa - it was just like meeting Santa Claus. I had a Golliwog, unfashionable now, to play with along with my teddy bear. The teddy bear, called Billy was acquired as you might say. One day on the way home from a shopping trip to town, I was in the pram and I spotted a teddy on a window ledge in Chester Road. My sister Rose at my request took the little fellow and gave it to me. I treasured it for years but if the rightful owner recalls their loss, I do now hereby apologise for the theft.

As I grew older I ventured further afield than Brocklehurst farm gate. I started with a walk to the end of Field Bank Road where there were a number of large concrete blocks, I understand now they were to be used to block the road with should Hitler's tanks ever get as far as Macclesfield. One of my favourite places was a large pond just off Arlington Drive where along with many other children I used to dabble in the water for tadpoles and newts which I would proudly take home in my 2lb jam jar with its string carrying handle.

It was on one of these excursions that I saw workmen taking down a chestnut paling fence opposite Arlington Drive and unloading some machinery. They were starting to build what is now Earlsway on the Weston Estate, named after the owner of the land, Macclesfield's MP at the time, Garfield Weston of Weston Wagon Wheels fame.

As I grew older and bolder my walks would go further to explore the countryside. Today a child is not allowed to go anywhere for fear of strangers but I used to walk all the way to Bluebell Valley, Henbury, at the junction of Bearhurst

Lane. In those days there would be many cyclists from places like Manchester who came to pick the bluebells. It was a common site to see bunches of bluebells hanging from saddlebags. Now the wood is surrounded by a holly hedge and a wire fence to stop the loss of these beautiful flowers which carpet our woods every springtime. I was to become a regular visitor to the farm next door as there was a boy of my age called John Brocklehurst.

At my primary school, apart from Miss Sheldon I recall Mrs Cotton and Mrs Steele who took the babies' class. The one who most influenced my life was Mrs Wardle who seemed very old but of course was not, when you are only desk high.

As well as *Wind in the Willows* I later read all the *Romany* books which I borrowed from the public library and I listened intently to children's hour on the radio to 'Wandering with Nomad'. Later in my life I visited Romany's caravan which was preserved to the rear of the Rex theatre in Wilmslow.

Everything seemed good to me, even our eviction was an adventure for me but more of that later. I was in fear of my father as a small child, but my mother took good care of me. My intense dislike of him probably equipped me later for a life of self-sufficiency.

Athey Street school. The juniors were on the ground floor, the seniors upstairs. It is now Park Royal school.

HOME AND WORK

From the moment I left school at the age of fifteen it was always my intention to be self-employed, an ambition which took me just a little longer than I had planned. I did not achieve it until I was twenty-six.

After a number of years at number 157 Chester Road my parents fell out and my mother, with me and my younger brother and sister, moved out for two nights to a one roomed house,1 Shaw Street (an end property later demolished following a fire). We moved back but eventually we were evicted for non-payment of the rent and had to move into a small flat above 12 Beech Lane.

We moved to a shop at 20 Cross Street which we rented from Mr and Mrs Pickford who sold greengrocery from the shop next door, number 22. The shop on the other side was a cobbler's occupied by Danny Norton a well-known figure in the community - he was amongst other things the bandmaster of the Cheshire Regiment band at the Drill Hall in Bridge Street.

My mother earned a living by buying and selling secondhand goods, mainly furniture. Just after the war these goods were in demand. I would often accompany her to one of the two sale rooms in the town where she would buy most of the stock - Brocklehurst's on King Edward Street and George Brian's on Great King Street.

It was not long before my parents had a further disagreement and my father with my two half-sisters moved to number 82 Cross Street and set up in opposition to my mother in another second hand shop. This did not last very long and my father exchanged the shop for a house in Union Street with a man called Berrisford. Many of the older readers may remember Charlie Berrisford as the little man who took photographs for the local papers. He was the one who took ages to set up the picture presumably because he always wanted to take only one because of the expense of film - or photographic plates - in those days.

Life was tough now but it was all I knew. The long walk to school made me very fit but I longed for a bicycle and one day my mother agreed subject to one condition - I was to have lessons on the violin. The instrument was provided by my Uncle Leslie and lessons started with an old man in Sunderland Street. The man insisted that his daughter, about my age, had lessons at the same time as me but I felt that as I was paying for the tuition I should not have to share with a girl I did not like. As a result I only lasted a few weeks and when I stopped, the bike went too. It was probably these hard knocks that made me determined not to be poor in life.

Things improved and we finally got a house of our own at number 193 Park Lane with my mother taking on a mortgage. It was a great place to live with a large garden to the rear and an entrance from Barton Street so we did not use the front door very often. The other big advantage was no neighbours. Both number 191 and 195 were occupied by doctors surgeries, Dr Mark, Dr Gillies senr, Dr Hart and Dr Tannenbaum.

Although still a schoolboy I was flushed with success when I passed the eleven plus exam and transferred to the Kings School. It was at this point in my life that my mother decided to revert to her maiden name so I became a Maddock and not a Ponting.

My first experience of work was when I took on a Saturday and Sunday job with the local milkman, Mr Bowers, who worked with a horse called Major and a two-wheeled milk float. My work was to pick up the various jugs from window ledges and bring them to the float where Mr Bowers filled them from a large milk churn with one of two ladles. One held one pint and the other half a pint. I would then return the jugs to the appropriate window ledges.

Sometimes the horse would move on without instruction as a number of the customers fed the horse with crusts of bread and the horse would often anticipate such a morsel. One must remember that at this time there were no cars in the streets, like today when you cannot move in the back streets for parked cars. In Barton Street where I lived we would regularly play football or cricket in the street and the only time we were disturbed was when the milk float came by.

My most treasured memory of this job was when I was allowed to take the reins and steer the horse across Park Green on the way to the dairy. There were no traffic lights in those days and very few cars, so it didn't matter that I was only about 12. The dairy was just off Windmill Street, above the railway bridge long since gone and made into a new factory. There was a second dairy we sometimes visited, in Davenport Street behind the Central railway station and next to Gleave Motors.

The job ended each day at a farm on Moss Lane, now Effluent Services yard. It was owned by the Stanier Brothers and farmed by a Mr Barnes. He had a daughter about my age to whom I was very attracted but I was always much too shy to talk to her but I made excuses to call at the house for a drink of water.

After we had cleaned the dairy and turned out the horse we fed the pigs from a large boiler in which the swill from various pig bins had been boiled. At the end of the day I was paid three old pence, but later it was raised to nine old pence. I could not save much on this so I looked elsewhere and found work as a paper boy in Brown Street, at the corner of Barton Street.

THE PAPER ROUND, EXTRACT OF ARTICLE MACCLESFIELD EXPRESS 25TH MAY 1994

I*n the early 1950s I was employed by Billy Lennard, newsagents in Brown Street, as a paper boy, being responsible for deliveries both mornings and evenings as well as two rounds on Sundays, one of which covered the Moss Estate. For this work I was paid the sum of twelve shillings and six pence per week. Every week I saved this* *money to buy myself a Raleigh Super Lenton bicycle with alloy wheels, G.B. brakes and Sturmey Archer four speed gears - all the very latest. This cost me thirty five pounds from Shackletons cycle shop on Church Street.*

One of my best memories of the job was that after school I got to take the shop bike, a very heavy machine with a large carrier on the front, and cycle down to Hibel Road railway station to meet the train carrying the evening papers. On the platform, along with the other waiting paper boys, we gave each other rides on the four wheel trolleys used by the staff to unload parcels from the trains. In charge was Mr Evans, a large rotund man who came from his home in Park Lane (one of the twelve apostles) in a small van. He sat firmly on one of the trolleys, his sole job, as wholesale newsagent for the town, to distribute the papers to the boys.

As the trains arrived the tunnel was filled with acrid black smoke which choked you for a few seconds, then as the train pulled to a stop all the doors would fly open as if by magic and scores of people would alight whilst others scrambled in the opposite direction. During the brief stop, the boys would note the name and number of the engine, while rail staff would quickly unload the mountain of parcels and our precious papers. We hurriedly ferried them to Mr Evans who counted out to each boy the allotted number and one by one we sped off on our bikes.

As I approached the shop a small crowd of men would be waiting, all milling around the shop entrance in eager anticipation of the latest news, delivered by me. There was no TV news then. There was a brief wait whilst Billy Lennard marked the addresses on each paper and then each boy would start off on his daily delivery - to the best of my knowledge there were no paper girls in those days. There must have been days when it was miserable and wet but I can only recall the good times when I brought the news to the good people of Macclesfield in the Brown Street area.

I also secured work through the school on the Royal Mail delivering the Christmas post on two consecutive years. As soon as I had finished my paper round each morning I would turn up at the sorting office in Castle Street/Derby Street, now part of the Cheshire Building Society, to start my round as a postman. On some days I worked so late that I had to go off on my evening paper round straight after my mail deliveries. I cannot remember how I managed to fit in time to eat but I suppose I did. Each day meant more cash to spend. I could not wait to leave school and start full time work.

I left before I was sixteen, which at the Kings school was the earliest age for leaving. If I had not, I may well have been expelled for continual truancy. I really did not like school and I often thought that it did not like me. I did not understand those who told me that school days are the happiest days of your life.

On leaving school my first job was as an assistant screen printer at Barracks Fabrics, Lower Heyes Mill on Black Lane. It was a dirty and hot, sweaty job which I detested but I stuck at it until I landed a much more suitable job.

It was not to long before I secured a good job at Firesnow Ltd on Withyfold Drive as a clerk, or assistant to the works manager a Mr Bond. I enjoyed the work and the responsibility of a nice clean job in the office with a certain amount of authority over the factory workforce.

WORKING DAYS, EXTRACT OF ARTICLE MACCLESFIELD EXPRESS 2ND NOVEMBER 1994

Although I was educated at the Kings School, and you were expected to remain in full time education until the age of sixteen, as one of five children from a one parent family, I could not wait to leave school and start work. I abandoned the school - or you could say that I left by mutual consent to avoid the possibility of my being expelled for persistent truancy at the age of fifteen years.

My first job was as an assistant screen printer at Barracks Fabrics at Lower Heyes Mill. The work was arduous and very hot in the steamy conditions. Whilst I liked the two men I worked with I did not like the job and was only too glad when I was offered a job around the corner with John Morris (Firesnow) Ltd. I worked there as an assistant to Derek Bond, the manager, until I was called away to do national service with the RAF.

On my return to the job after two years away I found the firm had had several managers, all unsatisfactory. This resulted in my landing a plum job by default. I found civilian life difficult and even more difficult was working for the managing director Mr Cedric Morris. I finally abandoned the attempt to get on with him and made applications for five different jobs. Jobs were plentiful in those days.

I was interviewed and offered all five posts but chose to accept a job as a wages clerk at Parkside Hospital. I enjoyed this job for nearly four years, paying the wages to the 650 staff who tended to the 2,000 patients. I eventually got a promotion to pay wages in the Wolverhampton area. After I left Parkside they installed their first computer to pay wages and they recruited two staff to replace me. Soon the number of staff had increased to 900 whilst the number of patients had dropped to 1,200.

I found living away from home in Wolverhampton difficult and I returned to the town to take a job with Conlowes of Congleton. But I was an ambitious person and I soon decided to be self-employed and opened a driving school. It was a great success and over the years I taught about 350 people with a first time pass rate of 85%. Later I moved into the coach business and took on the responsibility of carrying hundreds of children to and from school. There must be thousands who at one time or another travelled on one of my coaches.

During the next ten years of my life I managed between jobs to develop an interest in building. I started with walls and garages and progressed to houses. I am self taught but I have built the last four properties I have lived in. The second of these

The factory of Firesnow in Withyfold Drive where I started my career.

Me in RAF uniform at the start of my national service in November 1955.

The fire crew at Gaydon Airfield where I served for eighteen months.

houses was an experiment in self sufficiency and was televised twice on BBC's Look North programme. Our MP was quoted at the time as saying I was 'forty years ahead of my time'. No one wanted self sufficient houses then, not in 1980.

I am now semi-retired and turning thirty seven acres of land into a wildlife habitat where I can be away from the smoke and grime of the town centre. At school I had hoped to be an architect, not a bus driver, but the skills I learnt at school were not wasted. I am not thrilled with the world in which I live and I am endeavouring to leave it somewhat better than I found it. I wish everyone would do the same and stop exploiting the planet for personal gain - and leave something for the next generation.

Some ten years on from that article nothing has really changed, it's still every man for himself. Most of us are overpaid for what we do and few of us care what state we leave the planet in. The next generation will have to clean up the mess we leave behind us.

FIRESNOW - OLD MACC MAGAZINE JANUARY 2003

When I left the Kings School at the age of fifteen, after a short spell I secured a position as cost clerk and assistant manager of Firesnow Ltd., on Withyfold Drive. The manager at that time was Derek Bond.

I worked there until my country demanded my presence on National Service. After two years I returned but found things not to my liking. Firesnow Ltd. was a small company which made fire extinguishers and valves for coal mines. The owner was Cedric Morris, son of John Morris who ran the original business in Salford. Cedric's brother ran a similar factory near Chester. Cedric was a little man with a moustache like that of Hitler.

In the fifties Firesnow employed around fifty personnel, some of whom I remember with affection. Jim Thornley ran the buying department. He was a real gentleman who later worked behind the counter at Blackshaw's in Sunderland Street. The machine shop foreman was a man called Hill who was a fanatical football supporter. Mr Cowan ran the foundry and the man I remember the most was Seth Schofield the foreman in the paint shop.

All these memories came flooding back when I uncovered the aerial photograph of the works taken around 1954. Did you work at Firesnow? What are your memories of the old firm?

In November 1955 I was called up to do national service for my country and was given the number 2780418 and made an airman grade two in the Royal Air Force. I would have been one of the last to be called to do this service as it was abolished some weeks later. I had to report to RAF Cardington in Bedfordshire, the home of the British airships. After being issued with uniform and given the customary health check and haircut I, along with dozens of others, was shipped out by train to RAF basic training camp at Bridgnorth in Shropshire. Here I spent a miserable eight weeks square bashing and being shouted at in order to make me a man who could be relied upon in a time of war. Here I first met Brian Capper who lived in Northwich and we remain firm friends to this day.

From Bridgnorth I was sent to train as a fireman at the RAF fire-fighting school at Hull, for nine weeks. I enjoyed this training - it was a great honour to train as a fire fighter as I was the only national serviceman there, because of my previous employment at Firesnow.

At the end of this training I was sent, despite the fact that I already had a driving licence, to Weeton near Blackpool, the RAF driver training school. Here we learnt to drive and to maintain vehicles and over the next nine weeks I took and passed seven driving tests ranging from Landrovers to twenty-five ton fire fighting vehicles.

Being so near to Blackpool, and the start of the summer season, with little or no money, was a hardship. My weekly pay was twelve shillings and sixpence and I was expected to send money home! We really struggled to make ends meet. We begged lifts into town and cups of tea from the young girls serving in the cafes on the sea front - but this was not too difficult when in the uniform of the RAF.

I was now posted to RAF Gaydon in Warwickshire halfway between Leamington Spa and Banbury and close to the village of Kineton. This was very exciting as it was the number one crash strip in Great Britain, the most up to date airfield in the country. It was predominantly used as a training base for pilots flying the Valiant Bombers although at times we did have the Hanley Page Victors and the Avro Vulcans on the station. It was not unusual for aircraft from as far away as Germany to be diverted to us for a crash landing if fuel on board permitted.

During my time at Gaydon my rank was upgraded several times until I became a Senior Aircrafts Man and for doing an average sixty hour week on duty I was paid the princely sum of six pounds ten shillings per week. Although the security on the base was tight and we were not allowed cameras, I did manage to secure some cine film footage of the aircraft.

CLASSIC 999 MAGAZINE OCTOBER 2004

I trained as an aerodrome fireman driver in the RAF in the early part of 1956 and enclose a picture of a Thornicroft MkV, similar to the one in the August issue taken at the RAF training school. I am the fifth from the left on the middle row, seated next to the instructor. Note this vehicle does not have the monitor on the roof.

The vehicles were, from left to right, a Bedford water tender, a gas truck, a Thornicroft MKVa foam tender, and a rescue Landrover with dry powder extinguisher. This MKV differs from the one in the previous picture as it has a roof mounted foam gun and a much bigger grille. This vehicle had a Rolls Royce B81 petrol engine, and was later replaced by the MKVI, a six wheeler on an Alvis chassis.

The only time I was away from Gaydon was for three days when I had to go to RAF Daventry to check the fire equipment and train the personnel in fire fighting as the station was too small to have its own fire fighters.

As mentioned earlier, after my national service I soon found myself as a wages clerk at Parkside mental hospital. I worked alongside three colleagues, Albert Wrigley, Dick Hankinson and John Bennett and I really liked the work.

I became the treasurer of the hospital social club and in that capacity I had to organise the dances in the large hall. The dances attracted attendances of up to seven hundred people in those days and I was able to persuade some of the top bands to play for us. We soon raised enough money to build a social club which still stands today but is used by the Alzheimer's society.

I used to play cricket for the hospital second team although I think my selection owed much to the fact that I had a twelve seater minibus - handy for away matches.

In 1963 I was offered the opportunity to go to America for four months as a camp councillor at no cost to myself. You can imagine I jumped at the chance, but before I went I took a temporary summer job at Capesthorne Hall. I loved this outdoor work and the man who took me on, a Mr Beck, was very good to me. I was called upon to fell and plant trees, to clear drains and even to install a cattle grid.

Prior to my going to America I had been driving a Ford Consul which I now hired out so I would have some cash in the bank on my return. I had been using this car for rallying and teaching driving, and I had already decided that when I returned from America I would open up a driving school. But when I came home in November I found my lovely yellow car had been written off. With the insurance money I bought my first new car. I went to Horns in Chestergate, next to the old Drome Cinema, to buy the very first Vauxhall Viva in Macclesfield straight from the motor show and I used this to start my own driving school. I became a RAC registered instructor and with good test results and nice new cars, my business boomed - although I must thank the father of Ashley Hunter, an old school pal, who gave me a temporary job as a driver at Carswells Parcels in Black Lane whilst I built up the business.

Self employment proved a great success. It was time for a house move and as I had developed an interest in horse riding I wanted a place with some land. In 1968 a house on Windmill street came onto the market with a one acre paddock. At £6,000 my mother and I agreed to buy. After the sale was agreed the estate agents, pulled a dirty trick and produced another customer, a Mr Paddock of Saville Street Motors. We were forced into putting in sealed bids - Mr Paddock put in £6251 and I opted for £6,501 so I got the property. It seems very cheap now.

At this time I had plans to take the scouts abroad to Le Mans and Paris but the hire cost of a minibus was too high. I decided to purchase one from Johnny Platts on Waters Green for £350 on the condition that he bought it back on our return. As it

Two of my Vauxhall Viva driving school cars of the early sixties.

Jackie Cleworth on one of my driver training courses held at the boys' club in Oxford Road.

My Mercedes Coach at the National Coach Rally in 1973 where I won the Concours D' Elegance class.

turned out I was so pleased with it that I kept it and this set me on course for the coaching business.

I later purchased from Locomotors on Union Road a brand new blue Commer minibus and called myself Reliable Mini Coaches (my driving school was Reliable School of Motoring). The coach business took off as well and I soon purchased a new twelve seater, a Martin Walter conversion on a Transit chassis. My last new vehicle was built for me at Formby on a Mercedes chassis, and helped me win the 'Concorde d' Elegance' at the 1973 coach rally in Blackpool.

I purchased other secondhand minibuses and added them to my fleet and this helped me keep a monopoly in the business for several years. Then as the carrying of children to school became a greater part of my business, I found a loophole in the regulations and purchased two Commer coaches, a 35 seater and a 42 seater. I developed a strategy of making all my drivers self-employed and selling them the coaches to do the work under contract to me. I called the business Mecca Transport and by the time I retired I was carrying over one thousand pupils to school every day.

Once I had settled in my house in Windmill Street I planned to build a bungalow to the rear of the house. In this I was greatly assisted by the Council's architects department - it would not happen today. The new bungalow helped me to test my ability as an architect. It had under floor central heating and a patterned roof.

Once in the new bungalow I set about converting the house into three flats as a source of income. After only a few years I sold the property as a house again

Using some of the money from the sale I purchased an old mill with a cottage and four acres of land in South Wales. This property had been on the market for one and a half years. Despite the problems of travel I spent as much time as I could renovating the property and even got planning approval to convert the old corn mill to a dwelling but I was to receive an offer on the whole property which was too good to refuse so I sold.

I now decided to buy woodland in order to develop my interest in nature reserves. During the early eighties I lived for fifteen months in one of my old Commer coaches and a caravan whilst I built Ecolodge the country's first self sufficient house.

In 1982 the riding club, of which I was president, lost its right to use a field opposite the Star Inn on London Road and I was in a position to buy land when twenty one acres now known as Mecca came up for sale. I bought the land in order that the riding club would have a venue. I did not know or plan at the time of purchase that I would later build my present home on this site.

CONSERVATION PROJECTS

As I have mentioned previously I was greatly influenced by the *Romany* books and the *Wandering with Nomad* series on children's hour each weekday at five o'clock. In those days before TV, we all listened to the radio - in our case, Radio Relay, which gave us a choice of four programmes sent directly by wire from a shop situated on the corner of Chestergate and Westminster Street. How many can still remember listening to Dick Barton, special agent, with his sidekicks Jock and Snowey at seven in the evening. My most popular programme was Radio Luxemburg.

In my early teenage years, I along with my friend Robert Locket, made very regular trips on bicycle, to our favourite destination, Gawsworth. We would park our cycles behind the gravedigger's hut to the rear of Gawsworth Church and walk towards North Rode and Whalley Woods. Many a happy weekend was spent in those woods where we would build shelters and cook food over open fires.

Unfortunately, in those days, like many others, I was an egg collector. It was not an illegal activity then and we all thought that birds could not count so if we took one egg they would not miss it. You could also make up your collection by mail order.

Gawsworth was our favoured spot. I was a frequent visitor to Maggoty Johnson's Wood where Lord Flame was buried, the court jester to one of the King Henrys. There was a period in my life that I was known as the 'Squire of Gawsworth'. During a school holiday I got employment with a Mr Bailey on his farm at the Harrington Arms. He ran the farm whilst his wife ran the pub. That was in the days before the new road by passed it and when the pub floor was stone flags and the beer came from wooden barrels. It was a bus stop on the route to Crewe. Each year, Mr Bailey allowed the village rose queen fete and equestrian event to take place on the field opposite the pub. In addition to the gymkhana they had horse racing and on-course betting.

On one of our many visits to Whalley Woods we found a tawny owl's nest in which we found that the young birds were being fed on fish. That was a surprise to me as I had not heard that owls catch and eat fish. On one of our visits we witnessed the death of one of the parent birds. It may have been wrong but we took the two young owls home and I kept them as pets. I was very successful at their rearing and I often took them with me to South Park where I would fish from the pier with cotton and a bent pin to catch small fish to feed them.

The birds were kept in the coal shed and the dustbin man would not take our bin because he was afraid of the two birds sitting on the bin. I called the birds Tony and Tessa and as they grew older I used to release them into the park at night so they could hunt but they always came back. If I left my bedroom window open I would often awaken to find them both sitting on the rail at the bottom of my bed.

Tony and Tessa my Tawny owls who won first prize at the High School.

The birds became great celebrities and in May 1952 they won first prize as the most original pets at the Girls High School annual fete. The local press printed photographs and I appeared in the News of the World and the Picture Post.

Another project started in 1966 when I saw an advert for 4.16 acres of land for sale at Cess Bank Common in Higher Sutton. After much negotiation I secured the property for the sum of £168, a large amount in those days. The land was covered with heather and the previous owner had built a small summer house which was becoming very dilapidated. I spent many happy hours up there where the only sound you heard was of curlew, peewit and skylark. The small stone quarry on the site had been used by the local farmers as a dumping ground for their rubbish which included at least one old lorry chassis. As there was too much to remove I had the quarry filled in with spoil from the new Scragg's factory being built in Langley.

My plan was to rebuild the summer house in stone as I was assisting in the work of demolishing the Trinity Church in Cumberland Street opposite the old Infirmary. I carted several loads of the beautiful Kerridge pink stone and one of the church's interior doors up the long steep hill called Wythenshaw Lane to the site of the hut. My poor little black Austin A40 van struggled on those journeys and it was not long before the vehicle met its demise.

During this work on the church I was fortunate enough to meet Blaster Bates who had been brought in to demolish the spire. Blaster was well-known on the club scene as a guest speaker and he had also made a recording about his various exploits which had included the clearing of tree stumps for the new racing circuit at Oulton Park - he christened Knicker Brook.

THE CHURCH THAT WOULD NOT DIE OLD - MACC MAGAZINE APRIL 1999

In the days before the inhabitants of Macclesfield were deprived of their beloved infirmary, there stood in Cumberland Street a beautiful church complete with spire, known as Trinity Church. In those days Cumberland Street ended in a T-junction with Prestbury Road where the Park Hotel stood.

In 1967 the church was abandoned and during its destruction I was fortunate enough to be able to save one of the internal doors and some of the beautiful stone in which it had been built.

Once the body of the church had been removed the spire stood proud on its square base, somewhat out of place in splendid isolation. It was at this point, 15th November 1967, that I had the fortune to be able to work alongside the famous Blaster Bates who had been employed to demolish the spire with explosives.

Blaster turned up at 6am in his modest green Morris Traveller, with the explosives, detonators and wire strewn across the back of the car. The huge man extracted himself from his small car wearing camouflage from head to foot and looking every bit like a member of the SAS. He was an impressive man, over six foot tall and built like a rugby player but despite this appearance he was always in a jocular mood. He just loved to talk about his work and in particular his part in the construction of the Oulton Park Race Track just after the war.

On the morning of 15th November we drilled holes into the base of the tower and placed the charges. Once this had been completed the police closed the road to traffic and all the newspaper reporters and members of the public crouched down behind the wall of the infirmary opposite. I recall it was still dark, a very foggy morning and everything was extremely quiet. I positioned myself on a fire escape, with my camera in hand, to the rear of the spire at a factory in Riseley Street, and then waited for the bang.

Once Blaster had lit the fuse the only noise in the silence was the sound of Blaster's boots on the road as he hastily made his exit in the direction of the Park Hotel. He did not stop running until the enormous 'bang'. Dust shot up, pigeons flew out of the spire, and the iron cross on the top snapped off with the vibration and clattered down the outside of the building in the eerie silence.

As the dust settled and the public came out from behind the wall it slowly became clear in the fog that the spire still stood. Once Blaster had returned to the scene and the morning became lighter, we could see that two of the four walls at the base of the tower had been blown out leaving a hole big enough to drive a bus into. The spire was defying gravity and stood, just as it had done for many years, and long before the birth of Blaster Bates.

The police insisted on the site being fenced off as it was evident the spire was a little shaky - it could clearly be seen to move in the wind. It was resolved that a second attempt would be made at 7am next day.

A number of windows had been blown out of the adjacent building which was occupied by MAFF in those days and during the day a happy glazier replaced all the glass to the satisfaction of the staff who worked there.

The next day, well before daylight, Blaster and I set to work once more to place more explosive charges. When I suggested a little more explosive this time he said, "I can put enough in to blow the thing sky high but heaven knows where it would come down".

The procedure was the same as before: the police closed the road, pedestrians and photographers took cover behind the wall, Blaster lit the fuse and once again started his run in the silence, up Cumberland Street. Once again a loud 'bang', the evacuation of the spire by the pigeons and again, to everyone's amazement, the same result. An even bigger hole and a spire which waved even more in the breeze. But once again it defied gravity. We all began to wonder if God was trying to tell us something.

With much regret the employees of MAFF would once again face a day in a draughty office as no one had thought to board up the newly glazed windows. The police now insisted that Blaster should not leave the scene until the job was completed, so, with a great deal of caution, we set to and drilled more holes for more explosives in the base of the now extremely unsafe structure. This time, another loud bang .....and success as the spire crumpled into a heap in the space where the church had stood. The adventure was over.

The iron cross is all that remained of the spire and the tip of it still resides in a garden in Macclesfield, a proud trophy for Brian Ollier, who incidentally provided the only picture of the downfall of the spire. All those who took pictures on the first day were to be disappointed as the fog had reflected all the light from the flash bulbs into the camera lenses.

The site is now occupied by sheltered housing for the elderly. I wonder how many of them know of the events which occurred when I worked with Blaster Bates to see off one of Macclesfield's landmarks? Much as I enjoyed the excitement I often regret the loss of Trinity Church, as much as I regret the loss of the infirmary.

As a footnote you may recall in chapter one that it was this church from which my father stole lead from the roof.

As I grew older I started to read more about conservation and I was particularly impressed by the book by John Seymour called *Self Sufficiency*. It sparked an idea in my head that I would one day build a house which did not rely on services provided by the local council, one which produced all its own energy from the sun, the rain, or the wind.

My early experience at building, as a boy living in Park Lane around 1950, was when I tackled the eight foot stone wall at the rear of our house. We had just bought our first motor vehicle, a Standard Vanguard with a truck body and canvas hood, and needed somewhere to park it. On my own I felled two poplar trees and removed twelve feet of the high stone wall and made a rockery of the stone to enhance the garden. I then built up the ends of the wall - a very bad job as it turned out - although I was proud of the job at the time. It was my first step as a self-taught builder.

I had lacked the finance to put any of my ideas into practise but once I became self-employed things began to improve fast. With a coach business, not to mention an adventure into landscape gardening, to add to my driving school business I found that I could now afford a new project - although I would have to provide all the labour myself.

The house Shawleigh, I purchased in 1968, had land to the rear. Here I planned my first project. I would design and build myself a bungalow just to see if I could. This was the start of the house which became Pineleigh, a property with a new style under floor ducted central heating system like the Romans had, but unlike theirs it was gas fired, not by burning wood.

I started in 1970 and did almost all of the work myself and was very pleased with the resulting three bedroomed bungalow with a lovely patterned roof. As the VAT was reclaimable on a self build property, the whole project, including fitted furniture and carpets, came to only £4,500. A staggering figure compared with prices of property today.

I moved into the new house in the summer of 1973 and lived there for three and a half years until I decided to move on to something bigger and better. I sold the bungalow for £18,500. I also converted the large Shawleigh into three flats and for a while lived off the income from their rental. Some of my tenants were quite good but inevitably I found myself with a tenant who was not and I gave up the idea of being a landlord. I turned the flats back into a single dwelling and sold it to a man from Bristol who had just secured a post as deputy head at a local comprehensive school.

I was still intent on building myself a self-sufficient house. I managed to obtain some lovely stone from a wall around Forest Cottage, when it was demolished to facilitate the widening of the junction of the new and old Buxton Roads. Mr Poyser of Rainow also found me some stone from an old farmhouse he was demolishing in Bollington, and I secured large beams nine inches by six from the roofs of houses in Byron Street which John Hobson was in the process of clearing.

I first used it all to build myself a nice new stable block for my horses. After discussions with a local architect Rod Hackney (one time adviser to Prince Charles) the plans for my new house of the future were drawn up and cleared by the planning department of Macclesfield Borough Council.

With my bungalow sold, I was to live in one of my old coaches converted to living accommodation during the building phase of my new home. The work started with a very large hole in the ground which was to house the water tank in connection with the heating system. This and the all-glass roof, windmills and methane digester made it a unique property and the first of its kind in the country and as far as I am aware only the third in the world.

I called this house Ecolodge. It was the most publicised project that I have ever undertaken in my drive to make the world a better place. It was long in the planning and I visited an old quarry at Machynlleth in North Wales where a few like minded people had started a centre for alternative technology and I drew much of my inspiration from their work and planned that my house should be the most self sufficient in the country. Machynlleth is still thriving today and has very many more visitors.

At about the same time Granada television were planning a similar venture in Macclesfield to the rear of Upton Hall. I did offer advice but they were not interested as it was only being done as a television programme and not as a serious idea. Many of their ideas were very impractical. Brian Truman, the show's presenter, was only concerned with viewer ratings and the success of the project was not an issue. The windmill had to be taken down after only a few minutes filming as it was unstable. The solar roof panels were not practical as it was an open system which would have caused condensation in the building. This 'house of the future' may have been a success as a TV show but it was not in truth a practical house.

I was determined that I should not make the same mistakes - I wanted to live in my house of the future. Ecolodge had solar panels which heated water in a large underground tank to provide the heating, windmills on the roof to provide electrical power and a methane digester to change organic waste into gas for cooking. All the roof water was collected and used more than once by recycling. But I do not propose to bore you with pages of detail - if anyone is interested you can read a full account by George H. Armstrong published in several different languages by UNESCO in the July to September issue of IMPACT in 1979.

I held an open day during the construction stage when our MP Nicholas Winterton came and made a speech in which he said that I was *"forty years ahead of my time"*. There were many who showed an interest, the most pleasing were three professors from Leeds University who were studying the subject and asked many relevant questions.

Following my open day and its wide publicity a number of things happened. Most significantly in 1981 BBC television covered the venture in a programme called *Look North.*

During this period of my life came another event. I was elected to become the President of the Macclesfield Riding Club. Due to a change of ownership of the field the club had no place to hold their shows. I looked for land so that the club could survive and on the 4th June 1982 I managed to purchase twenty two acres of land formerly part of Tollets Farm. I later called it Mecca - but at the time I did not know how significant this purchase would become.I called it Mecca for Macclesfield

The Open Day at Ecolodge in 1981, with Nicholas Winterton.

Some of those present when Nicholas Winterton said I was forty years ahead of my time.

Equestrian Centre for Cultural Activities and also because I renamed my coach business, Macclesfield Elite Coach Club Administration.

Later, when the riding club moved away to a new venue in Bollington, I had to decide what to do with the site and the small buildings I had erected. I decided to try for planning permission to build a house on the site and work the land as a registered agricultural holding.

By this time Ecolodge was turning out to be, as predicted by Nicholas Winterton, forty years ahead of its time! The value of the land on which it stood became greater than the value of the house and stables that stood on it. I sold it and it became Braeside and now sports six very nice bungalows. I moved up to the 'shed' at Mecca as it was sometimes called and once again got used to cramped living space. But every brick and every piece of wood or glass from Ecolodge were recycled into something useful on the new site.

On the 1st June 1986 the fifteen and a half acres of land opposite Mecca came up for sale as the farmer was moving to Devon. I purchased this land, originally part of Tollets Farm, so I was bringing together land which had been split up over the years. In 1989 I successfully forced the power company to remove the six poles across this land and route the electricity supply underground. I wished to make the plot of three separate fields with ditches in between into one large meadow. I spent a lot of time infilling the hollows and clay pits in order to improve the field and during an eighteen month period all the spoil from two building sites was tipped there.

Once the site was levelled and reseeded I was able to take a silage crop off it every year and graze sheep there. Then the forestry were offering 100% grants for planting of new woodland. I made a successful application and in November 1995 I turned the field into 'Rayswood'. In order to celebrate the planting I again called on my friend Nicholas Winterton to plant an oak tree at an official ceremony. The opening was attended by the forestry commission and a number of local dignitaries

The new woodland has proved a great success and over the weekend of the 2nd and 3rd of May 2004 we held our first open day when the public were allowed to see the extent of the new reserve. The local park rangers organised conducted walks through the wood's one mile of tracks. The event was co-ordinated by my niece Susan Marsh to raise funds for Age Concern, East Cheshire. Once again my good friend, now Sir Nicholas, attended and supported the afternoon.

This new nature reserve, only ten years old, already supports an abundance of wildlife. I have seen badger, fox, stoat, mole, and of course, rabbit. Birds like heron, tawny owl, pheasant and wood pigeon frequent the wood. There are many species of butterfly and numerous plants I am not qualified to identify but it has recently been surveyed. I hope for many years to come to be able to look after this treasure and make it one of the best new woodlands in the borough.

On the 31st December 1986 I moved up to Mecca to reside in the 'shed'. I was

Some of the thousands of tons of infill used to level the fields before the planting of Rayswood.

The official opening of Rayswood by Nicholas Winterton on the 2nd December 1995.

planning a new house but I had to fight the council through two appeals to be allowed to build it in the green belt. I started work on 11th March 1990 before planning was approved - I had the firm intention to go ahead and build whatever the outcome of my appeal!

I was very disappointed by two councillors who visited the site on 8th August 1989 and promised to back my proposal. When in council they reneged on that agreement and voted against me. How can one trust a politician? Once I got the go ahead I quickly completed the work and I moved into my new home on 4th October 1991 where I live today and hope to spend the rest of my life here.

I now used up some of the surplus stone I had accumulated around the place to build myself a 'necropolis', a place of burial. Some say it is morbid but I just regard it as good forward planning. It has a nice lined tomb below and it is topped off with a weather vane depicting old father time, a copy of the one which tops the pavilion at Lords cricket ground. Around and shielding my home from the main road I have developed an arboretum of decorative trees. Both my horse of twenty eight years, Snoopy, and my dog of fourteen years, Lucky, now rest quietly in this piece of woodland.

I would like to mention another story at this point - the 'Nuns Hats'. Some years ago the Macclesfield Borough Council gave themselves planning approval to erect new market stalls next to the Town Hall in a conservation area. The plans were objected to by all of the heritage bodies as inappropriate but they went ahead anyway. The press had a field day and called the new stalls Nuns' Hats as they were made of white fibre glass and looked just like them.

Some years later the same councillors decided to build a new Town Hall extension which meant the removal of the market stalls. The work of demolition was given to a local firm who were planning to dump them in a landfill site and by chance, through a friend, they were offered to me as a gift. I accepted it willingly and they were put in a field at Mecca.

The council were not best pleased and tried to force me to remove them. My continual refusal upset them even more and caused them further embarrassment as the press had a field day. It was not long before their legal department got involved and served notice of enforcement on me. By now I had used the shelters to roof in my sheep handling pens at the rear of my house. When the matter came before an inspector on 21st July 1992 it was judged that despite the council arguments, I was within my rights to use them as such.

I felt it was a good case of recycling. I held an open day for the new shelters and invited the mayor and councillors to attend but none of them replied!

Another conservation project I got into also involved woodland. I saw an advert in the local paper for woodland for sale in the middle of Pott Shrigley Hall Hotel golf course, and I put in an offer. My bid was not accepted but some months later the estate

The first Open Day held at Rayswood on the 2nd and 3rd May 2004, organised by staff from Age Concern, Susan Gater organiser, Dominic Anderson, Linda Bennett and Mandy Hill, with assistance from the Rangers, Christine Robinson and Ray Weaver.
Also in the picture, Raymond Maddock and guest Sir Nicholas Winterton.

The famous 'Nuns Hats' used as sheep shelters, to the annoyance of Macclesfield Borough Council.

agent telephoned to say they had another wood in Pott Shrigley - was I interested?

I knew the area well in connection with my coach business. The woodland was known as Holme Wood and was right in the centre of the village and consisted of mature beech and sycamore trees. I was interested and put in a low offer but it appears that mine may well have been the only one. It was accepted on behalf of the inland revenue who I understand were acting on behalf of the receivers.

I secured ownership in July 1997 and had it surveyed professionally by a reputable firm from Halifax. On their recommendation and with the full agreement of the forestry commission I made plans to fell 68 trees and to establish new growth in the long term interest of the wood as a whole. As the wood was protected by a tree preservation order, something I did not know at the time of purchase, there was soon opposition to my plans.

The Parish Council muscled in to show the villagers they were doing their job. They were just a sideshow really but they put in their two pennyworth with a visit assisted by the forestry commission. In order to placate them the number of trees marked for felling was reduced to fifty one. Despite this some villagers started a petition and letters appeared in the press accusing me of destroying the wood for money. They were wrong. I attended a public meeting to explain the plans and this did stop most of their objections.

I now secured a grant from the forestry toward the cost of rebuilding the drystone wall around the woodland. When all this was completed I decided the wall along the highway boundary also needed to be rebuilt but there was no grant toward this work and as there was not enough stone, I needed to lower the wall from five feet to four.

Macclesfield Borough Council once again stuck their oar in and told me I could not touch the wall without planning permission. I tried to ignore them. It was my wood, my wall, and my stone and I would do what I liked. I even considered, as an act of revenge, selling all the stone and replacing the wall with wire but the council backed down and agreed that the lowering of the wall could be considered as a repair which would not need any planning approval. Another poke in the eye for self opinionated officials who should be forced to wear big pointed hats.

When the wall was finished everyone said how much better it looked. I then proposed to put a gate in it to gain access for the felling programme now agreed and upgrade the existing track through the wood. Once again the men from the council intervened. I needed exact plans for the new upgraded track giving precise levels at every stage of its construction. I need planning approval for a new access - I should pull down the wall and rebuild it after the trees were removed. They were wrong - it only applied to a new access onto a classified road and this road was not classified.

Needless to say I just ignored the idiots and did the work anyway. Having put in the gate I upgraded the track. Both objectives were reached and I have not heard a word from the council on the matter since.

Holmwood, Pott Shrigley, in spring 1998 with my dog Lucky having a day out.

An aerial view of the wood in Pott Shrigley.

I now needed to remove some of the soil and rubbish from behind the wall as over the years the accumulation was pressing on the wall. I also needed to cut down scrub trees growing under the wall. I was told they were covered by the trec preservation order. They were not - they would have to be at least six inches in diameter at a height of five feet to qualify. The council fought this point, once again at great public expense and we went to an appeal. The outcome was that I could remove the scrub trees.

When the work started to remove the detritus from behind the wall, with a digger on the inside and a lorry on the outside, once again a public official came along to spoil the party. The drivers were told to stop the work until such time that traffic lights were put in to control the few vehicles which were passing. Fortunately I arrived just after this little man had left and told the drivers to ignore him. I stayed on site to await the promised return of this official of the highways department but he did not arrive and the work was finished without traffic lights. I think, had he returned I might have punched 'jobs worth' on the nose - then I would have been in trouble!.

Whilst all this was going on there was a local campaign in the letters page of the local paper to stop the felling of the fifty one trees already agreed to by all parties. I will not refer to all the letters as most of them were stupid but I must mention one letter in particular. That was the one headed *'Planners let us down'* and penned by no other than Bollington's Town Mayor. I quote the first half of her letter in the Macclesfield Express.

So, We have to believe that we do not have enough money, as a borough to fight unacceptable planning developments?

This must be the same logic behind the proposed decimation of Holme Wood, Pott Shrigley. Residents are being told that the felling of 55 healthy forest trees is good forestry control. Responsible ownership, with no real financial gain, with a commercial value of £1,000 per tree? Pull the other one.

I had to reply to this letter in order to show how wrong the mayor was. My letter to the express was headed 'FELLING ESSENTIAL TO REGENERATE WOOD'.

In reply to Bollington's town mayor's letter I would quote part of the independent survey which the Forestry Commission, Macclesfield Borough Council, and two members of Pott Shrigley Council all had access to for a year before they made their decision on the trees selected for felling.

"The woodland is now very mature and the present crop of trees are becoming unwieldy in many instances. Some of these are likely to become dangerous in the near future because of increasing size and weight.

*I*n order to perpetuate the nature of this woodland, regeneration is now necessary and a phase of felling, thinning and replanting will ensure the continuity of this wood as a pleasing feature in the landscape."

With regard to her remarks that the value of each tree is £1,000, it is ridiculous. The value of useable timber in a tree varies between £1.50 and £1.80 per cubic foot dependent on market conditions, at present at an all time low. The trees selected for felling, some of which are already dead or dying, are on average 92 cubic feet in volume making them worth between £138 and £166 each, and one must take into account the cost of extraction on this difficult site.

If J. Tunstall can find me a customer who will pay me £1000 per tree I will donate 50% to the school in Pott Shrigley. If Bollington's Mayor is correct then the school could profit by some £25,000.

Needless to say I heard no more from her. It is a shame that councillors do not stick to things they know something about.

In the end the cheapest quote I could find to extract the 51 trees was greater than the value of the timber. I would have been out of pocket to the tune of £1,500. This and the unjustified opposition from the locals caused me to abandon any further works on the planned nature reserve. I later sold the wood to two of the locals whose houses backed onto the wood and let them have the problem and expense of its upkeep. People now started to remark on just what a good job I had done and how much better the approach to the village now looked. Even the Parish Council had to agree it was a great improvement but I never got any thanks or an apology from the self appointed opposition. Not even the mayor.

Now came my finest achievement in the field of conservation. I had been looking for the chance to buy woodland and not always with a great deal of success, as you can see. Then Withington Estates were selling off by auction some five parcels of woodland, I understand to pay death duties to the revenue following a death in the family.

On the 19th November 1998, having already inspected the various lots of woodland, I attended the Royal George Hotel in Knutsford and awaited the auctioneer. I was especially interested in two lots, separated only by a public footpath, referred to in the catalogue as Whitecroft Dean and Deans Rough, being 5.67 and 7.97 acres respectively. I had set my limit at £18,000 for the first lot and £24,000 for the second.

When the bidding started I sat and awaited my chance to join in and when the bidding seemed to slow down at £17.250 I put in my first bid. This was followed by a bid of £17,750 so I put in my second and final bid of £18,000 and awaited the outcome. It seemed like forever but the hammer came down and I became the owner of a wood.

The adjoining wood was of course of lesser interest to the other bidders as I had already the first. Even so the bidding rose steadily but at my bid of £17,250 the others all dropped out and I felt very pleased with my day's work. After the auction I was approached by a resident of the area and asked what was my intention with regard to the wood. I felt the urge to say that it was to become a caravan park, but I resisted and told them it was to be a nature reserve. They seemed relieved.

On closer inspection I found that in 1985 three new blocks had been planted as a cash crop. One of lodge pole pine and two of larch. There were some twenty six small pools on the map of the site, all silted up, very overgrown and acidic, supporting little wildlife. On further inspection and by viewing aerial surveys that I had done I discovered an additional pool not shown on the map. The woodland was so dense that each time I wandered into it I came out at a different point making it difficult to get a clear picture of what I had purchased.

I formulated a plan which would involve the felling of the pines and the thinning of the larch, removing every third row. I would join up seven of the small pools into a large pool with an island and on the other side of the public right of way join up eight of the smaller pools to form a second lake with its own island.

My research showed that all these pools had been marl pits. The farmers would dig out the marl and spread it on their fields as a fertiliser. As each pit filled up with water they would just dig another one. Regrettably at least two of these pools had been used as refuse pits and I had to spend a lot of time removing what was mostly bottles.

As there was no grant money available for this sort of work I approached the Manchester Airport Trust's Community Fund for support. I thought that the fuel from passing aircraft over many years was contributing to the damage caused to the top of many of the trees and the airport should contribute from the vast profits they were making. All went well and I was very optimistic that they would support the local community.

The inspection was carried out by Councillor Rab Parry. He showed no interest in what I was saying and spent the whole inspection birdwatching through his binoculars. He made no comments to me, unlike the pleasant lady who accompanied us on the day. His report put an end to any hope I had. A miserable man.

Despite this set back my plans were put into action. I employed a firm recommended by the forestry commission to do the felling and remove the rhododendrons. Four men with three chain saws, a tractor and a trailer, spent sixteen days in the wood after which it was at last possible to see the wood for the trees. The work produced three full loads of timber for the pulp mills but this was not enough to cover the cost of the felling.

I then found a local firm, Don Bradley to spend three weeks creating the two new lakes. The three machines he bought with him were huge. One called a swamp master was twelve feet wide across its tracks and we had to move a gate post to get it into the wood. Despite its massive size and weight it could move over the boggy ground with ease, even where you would lose your Wellingtons if you tried to walk there.

Weeks were spent creating a car park and some additional felling and planting. The sea of mud soon recovered and a sea of green took its place. The finishing

An aerial view of the new nature reserve in Lower Withington now called Whitecroft Dean.

The official opening of Whitecroft Dean Nature Reserve by Nicholas Winterton on the 8th August 2000.with the Mayor, Councillor G.Walter Wright, and Mayoress.

touches included four new access gates and some hardcore to improve the public way. I did some wild flower planting and stocked the new lakes with frog and toad spawn, fish and newts. In the first season Canada Geese nested on both islands and raised chicks. I invited the Cheshire Conservation Trust to look at the newly refurbished woodland with a view to making it a gift to them - but they refused the gift.

The project had cost me just over £17,000 not including my time. The Forestry Commission came up with a grant of just over £10,000. The neighbours were all very pleased but not the planning department of Macclesfield Borough Council. Once they got wind of what was going on they arranged for an old enemy of mine to see if I had breached any planning regulation. He came up with letters telling me that planning approval was needed for much of the work I had done. He was wrong of course - so I just ignored him. I did however write to him and express an opinion which is not suitable for the book. I am sure I am no longer on his Christmas card list! I did not care - my plans had been completed and I did have the support of the parish council.

On the 8th August 2000 I held an open day and my good friend Nick Winterton again agreed to unveil a plaque in the wood. I also invited the Mayor Walter Wright, a farmer by profession and they both enjoyed the day. I had a chance to discuss the council with both of them and I never heard from the council again on the matter. Good old Walter.

When I retired I found the work involved in maintaining one hundred and eleven acres too taxing - not to mention the problems the inland revenue were causing me with self assessment. I came to a decision to sell off most of my land and just keep the thirty seven acres close to home.

I imposed a condition on the deeds of the wood, now called Whitcroft Dean Nature Reserve, which restricted all activity detrimental to the flora and fauna of the wood. Mr and Mrs Webster who had only a short while before purchased the only property which adjoined the wood agreed to buy the wood with the conditions I had imposed. I have visited the wood several times since the sale and they are keeping it just as I would have wanted.

The Country Landowners Association, of which I am a member, wrote an article about my activities, a four page colour article in their national magazine. The local paper followed with a full page spread on my work and this lead to an interview with Paul Heiney for a half hour programme on radio four. The interview was broadcast on radio four on the morning of Sunday, 11th March 2002 in 'On your farm'. Fame at last.

SCOUTING

From the age of eleven years I found myself alternating between St. John's Sunday school in South Park Road, and the Newtown Methodists in Hatton Street depending on which of the two was having the best Christmas party or the best summer outing. On one trip we were walked to the railway station in Macclesfield and caught the train to Bosley from where we walked to a small field to the rear of the Queens Hotel on the A523 at Bosley. We played games in the sun, and ate jelly and ice cream and potted meat sandwiches.

Neither had a scout group, so I soon joined the 7th Macclesfield Brunswick Troop which met at the Chapel in Chapel Street. The scoutmasters were Billy Richardson and Phil Tittensor. Billy had been a scout since 1907 when scouting first started. I was so enthusiastic I was very soon promoted to patrol leader of the Peewit patrol. The other patrol leader was Les Crone who later went on to own the flower shop on Mill Lane where the new Silk Road now ends.

As a small group they did not go camping but to my great joy we were invited to go to camp with the scouts of Sutton St. James. This was a week in North Wales just outside Bangor at Glasinfryn. I will always be grateful to George Foot for my first experience of camping. On one particular day we had a great storm and the tent in which my patrol lived was badly torn. My first reaction was to go to George. He had enough problems of his own at that time and he swore at me and told me that as patrol leader it was my problem. So I went to the farm and found a large post and a maul, I drove the post into the ground next to the tent and tied the tent to it and it survived the rest of the week. It certainly taught me to do things for myself and not to rely on others - one of the finest lessons I ever learnt. Thank you George.

The rest of the camp was delightful. The driver of the train which crossed the viaduct next to the camp always sounded his hooter and waved to us when he passed. On the other side of the camp was a narrow gauge railway to the slate quarry and we used this to get a lift to the woods where we cut wood for the fires. This little train would stop and let us load the wood and stop again to unload it at the camp. I doubt safety regulations would allow this now.

At the age of fifteen I left Brunswick to join the newly formed group at St. John's where the scouters had never actually been scouts, so I effectively became acting scoutmaster at the age of fifteen. During my years at St. John's I went to Gilwell Park for my wood badge and later represented England as a camp councillor in America, and the group and scout band won every trophy in the association at least once. I organised camps and gang shows - there must be hundreds of you out there who would have been involved at one time or another.

During my time the parents' committee purchased the hall, 'Mafeking', from the diocesan authority. Later the church was demolished and a new church built on Weston Estate. The new church has now been demolished itself and replaced with a more traditional building - I wonder if this one will out-last the scout hall in South Park Road?

When I became old enough I was to take on the title of scoutmaster. People I recall from then were Johnny Blackburn, Maurice Brown, George Brown, Wilf Grainger, Graham Lockett and Roy Barton. There may have been others but I cannot be sure of my memory these days.

The following are a few dates from old diaries. In April 1959 the leaders attended a special conference at a school in Sale near Altrincham. In May 1959 the scout band performed at the scout rally held at Devisdale near Chester. Harry Pleeth was made the new district commissioner for scouts at a ceremony in our scout hall on the 9th September 1959. In September of 1962 I attended a conference at a holiday camp in Skegness when the guest speaker was Patrick Moore, of 'Sky at Night' fame. In April 1963 I attended a weeks course at the main training camp at Gilwell Park and this resulted in my wood badge, a particular honour not given to all and something of which I am rightly proud.

One of the most recognisable things about scouts is that they go camping, something I did an awful lot of from the age of eleven.

COMING A CROPPER AT THE CHAIN AND GATE BEND
MACCLESFIELD EXPRESS 13TH JULY 1994

There were many periods in my life spent camping, some with the scout group in places like Garn near Porth Madoc, Wray Castle on the banks of Windermere and local sites like Butterlands farm in Wincle and Nettlebeds Farm also in Wincle. This was in the days before the Barnswood camp site in Rushton which I was involved with from its early days. The most memorable camps would be the ones I spent with Roy Barton, when we would just take off at the weekends at the drop of a hat and go just where the fancy took us.

I well recall one such weekend as we had spent some time doing up an old tandem. For those too young to remember, a tandem is a bicycle made for two people. We also built a four wheeled trailer to pull behind the tandem to carry all our camping gear. The tandem was great fun, we even had a portable radio strapped to the trailer and at one time we experimented with a two way radio even though we sat only inches apart.

The first incident occurred as we were speeding past the Chain and Gate on the Congleton Road, before they had straightened out the road, when half way round the bend the trailer turned turtle and we dragged it several yards before our wagon train

Mafeking Hall, South Park Road, headquarters of the 9th Macclesfield St. John's Scout Group.

A Gilwell Park training group. I am the one on the right, seated.

came to a halt. Fortunately the radio still continued to play despite its unpleasant encounter with the rough road surface.

Our usual plan was to ask the farmer to find us a little work in exchange for eggs and milk and sometimes even bacon or rhubarb. On one such occasion at Pettywood Farm, Middlewich we got more than we bargained for. It was the weekend off for the farmer's hired hand and on the Sunday morning the farmer, Mr Small, got up with severe back pain. We offered to do the milking for him of the ninety head of Fresians. With machines of course, not by hand. I well remember it to be the hardest day's work I have ever done and when we had finished we spent the rest of the day asleep.

Our camp sites were always used as a base camp, a jumping off point for other adventures further afield. One of those outings took us by bike to Crewe Park where we enjoyed boating on the lake and sitting around in the sun. On another occasion we took the train from Middlewich station via Crewe for a day trip to Prestatyn.

I have many very happy memories of those weekends. We often used to ride in to Middlewich on our tandem and at the time a number of Irish navvies were digging a trench alongside the Sandbach Road. Every time we passed they would jump out of their trench and shoulder their shovels or picks and salute us as we rode by. Little incidents like this were what made life worth while. I do not see the youth of today enjoying such simple pleasures. It seems to me that in this violent world where life is lived at a hectic pace, no one seems to have time to enjoy life properly.

St John's had many days of happy camping which started in 1955 at a local site called Butterlands Farm, the home of the Goldstraws in Wincle. On one occasion at an Easter weekend camp, the seniors set off with all the heavy gear on a trek cart to walk the long uphill journey to Butterlands Farm. The night was dark and it was snowing heavily when we left Macclesfield. As a precaution we attached a tilley lamp to the axle of the trek cart, something not acceptable today. The rest of the troop would join us next day with two further trek carts.

As we were cold and tired we stopped at the Ryles Arms for a refreshment break but the landlord would not let us in and he only reluctantly sold us crisps and minerals. We pressed on and made camp before midnight and settled into our sleeping bags. When we got up next morning we found that the fresh milk in the billy can had frozen and this was inside the tent in which we had slept. I suspect that this toughened up some of these lads I was training and an experience they would not soon forget.

In 1961 the Poynton Scout Group were moving to new purpose-built headquarters and our group was given their old hut which had stood for several years on a site now occupied by a filling station on the main road through Poynton. We dismantled the hut and with great difficulty transported it to Wincle where we rebuilt it on a site next to Shell Brook on the land of Roger Lomas at Nettlebeds Farm. Many of the old boys will remember the happy hours we spent building it and then spending weekends there.

A camp at Wincle 1955, Butterlands Farm. The names of those I remember are Michael Fytton, Maurice Brown, Roy Barton, Jim Rose, Geoff Sherratt, and my brother Kenneth.

Philip Morton troop leader congratulates Elvin Birch on receiving his scout cord, whilst Paul Bamford, Christopher Carbery and Steven Ridgeway look on.

Wincle 1955 from left to right. Graham Lockett, Kenneth Maddock, Wilfred Burgess, Geoffrey Sherratt, and Roy Barton.

May 1963 when I invested a young Christopher Davenport, flanked by Graham Wilson and Philip Morton.

Apart from the local camps we always had a larger event annually and in 1959 and 1960 we travelled by Bartons coach to a site in North Wales near to Criccieth called Garn Dolbenmaen. On the first visit the villagers held a dance in our honour at the village hall and the following year we had a sports event when our lads competed against the village children. I think that the locals beat us quite easily.

In 1961 our annual camp was held at Cilan Farm, Llandrillo near to Bala Lake, and in July 1962 we travelled to Wray Castle on the shores of Lake Windermere. Despite the heavy flooding it turned out to be a very good week's camp for all.

Camping at Wray Castle, Windermere, in 1962. The picture includes Paul Mackay, Brian Smith, Graham Wilson, Philip Morton, and David Potts.

In 1964 we set our sites much higher and travelled abroad to camp, something I think at that time only the 2nd Bollington Group had done before. Our first trip was to Paris, where on arrival we stayed in a school closed for the summer break, and equipped with camp beds in the main hall. No supervision and no locked doors, we were free to come and go as we pleased. The place was called Lycee Michelet Vanves and was just outside Paris. Whilst we were there we were given invitations to attend the Bastille Day celebrations and the grand parade up the Champs Elysee under the watchful eye of General De Gaulle.

SCOUTING ABROAD WITH GENERAL DE GAULLE
MACCLESFIELD EXPRESS 26TH OCTOBER 1994

During my period as scoutmaster at St. John's I started an interest in camping abroad. Our first trip was to Paris where we stayed in a school on the edge of the city. I purchased a second hand minibus from Johnny Platt for the sum of £380 and Mr Platt kindly agreed to buy it back on our return. I liked the vehicle so much that I kept it and it was this vehicle that got me started in the coach business in 1968.

The most eventful part of our first trip was being invited by General De Gaulle to attend his parade (in a special area opposite his saluting base) on Bastille Day. We arrived at eight in the morning when the temperature was already in the seventies and getting warmer. I recall that the parade lasted for several hours as we watched and filmed mile after mile of military vehicles and cavalry pass along the Champs Elysee.

This trip was followed by one to Le Man where we stayed as guests of other scouts. Our trip coincided with the 24 hour race and we happily attended as special guests. The highlight of that visit was a special night out. Arrangements had been made to close a small café to the public for the evening and the local scouts and ourselves sat down to a special eight course meal which lasted from eight o'clock to midnight.

In later years there were trips to Spain and Portugal taking in bull fights in Madrid and Zaragossa. Then to Austria where we visited all the locations around Salzburg where the Sound of Music was filmed. We even managed to take in Vienna and Venice.

The last of our epic scout trips abroad was a tour of Scandinavia where we were headlines in the local paper in Trondheim on the edge of the Arctic circle. From the reception we received, I guess we must have been the first scout group to travel so far north, to the land of the midnight sun. The rest of the tour took in Oslo and the Kon-tiki raft exhibition, Stockholm and its royal palace, the famous mermaid and the Tivoli Gardens of Copenhagen. Our tour returned via Germany and Holland.

I expect the lads will remember it well: Philip Morton, Derek Smith, Graham Wilson, Christopher Carbery, Harry Royal, and Stephen Murphy. This was in the days when travel was not as easy as today and well before the Common Market.

All local scouts will have heard about their campsite at Barnswood just over the county border in Staffordshire. After all these years there will not be too many scouts who will know about its beginning. In February 1963, myself, along with Jim Rose

The scout tour of Scandinavia resting in Copenhagen with Christopher Carbery, Derek Smith, Philip Morton, Graham Wilson and two others.

and Adam Hope, were invited by Eric Whiston to go to Barnswood and look at the site as the owner was considering making it a gift to the scout association. We considered it an ideal site and it was accepted on 25th April 1963.

I was amongst those who started the initial work on the site which was heavily overgrown with rhododendrons. The only building was an old summer house, badly in need of repair. We spent many nights in that old hut cooking sausages over an open fire. I do not claim to have done much of the work that followed - much has been done since my time to the credit of all those who came after us. The camp must now be one of the best around and attracts many visitors. It must be very difficult today to run it with all the health and safety regulations which did not apply in my day. It is indeed a credit to the association.

In 1957 the World Jamboree was held at Sutton Coldfield in Warwickshire to celebrate fifty years of scouting and St. John's group sent two boys, my brother Kenneth and Roy Barton. The other representative from Macclesfield was Len Wood from the 1st Hurdsfield group.

I visited the camp on the 5th August and stayed overnight returning late the following day. The night I stayed a great storm flooded several sites and boys were evacuated to higher ground. I must say that I slept through it all. Whilst I was there I took lots of cine film on super eight colour film. I was fortunate enough to get pictures of the Queen and the Duke of Edinburgh and to see the Prime Minister. An outing I shall never forget.

My last memory was a milestone in my life. Following my wood badge at Gilwell I was chosen to be one of only two scouts to go to the United States as a camp councillor. The operation was organised on a large scale by the Committee of friendly relations amongst foreign students, of the YMCA.

I sailed from Southampton, 18th June 1963, on an Italian ship called M.S. Aurelia. That night was very stormy and the sea was rough, so the ship did not dock and we were sent out to the ship by tender. I recall that as I walked across the walkway from the small boat to the larger vessel, passengers from France were leaning over the ship's rail and being sick. Not a good start to the trip.

I spent the first few days in my cabin suffering from 'mal de mer' and the cabin steward fed me on dry bread and bananas. But I got my sea legs once we were out in the Atlantic and I joined the hundreds of other students in the many activities which cemented relations between nations. Many of those on board were, like me, to be camp councillors not only in scout camps but in others such as tennis schools. There were also many American students on board returning from their studies in Europe during their summer vacation.

The boat provided good meals and a plentiful supply of red wine at every meal. There were many parties as students of all ages and nationalities got together to exchange stories and experiences. The crossing of the ocean was slow but fun. On 27th July, early in the morning we spotted through the mist the unmistakable outline of the Statue of Liberty at the entrance to New York harbour.

After passing through customs and leaving all our new friends I, along with my mate from up north, caught the bus for Baltimore, the largest sea port on the east coast. As we travelled in an air-conditioned coach, with an air-conditioned bus terminus, it was a shock when we went out onto the street. The temperature was 104 degrees and it hit you like a wall. Sweat just started to run off us even if you did not move.

A car was sent to pick us up and we arrived at our destination, Broad Creek Scout Camp in Whiteford Maryland USA. The place was massive, even the lake was three times the size of Barnswood camp at home. It consisted of about thirty separate camp sites and I was to live in a tent close to the headquarters building. I had a bed, I did not even have to sleep on the floor. I was welcomed by 'Uncle Joe Hilderbrant' the camp leader. My tent mate, Bart Kelso of the Eastern Baptist College of St. Davids and I became very good friends.

My over-riding memory of the camp and especially of the nature lodge was the snakes. I have always disliked snakes. I was even more worried when, one day on the camp, a nest of Copper Heads was discovered, the largest was some forty two inches long, a record for the area. The other thing which shook me was that the instructor in weapons carried a six gun.

My job was just to walk about and talk to the boys. Each week there would be a new intake spread over many camp sites and I was in continuous demand. The most frequent questions asked were *'do you take tea each day at five o'clock?'* and *'do you have television in England?'* I usually answered this question in a jocular fashion saying that TV was invented by a Scotsman called Yogi Bear (Logie Baird).

I attended many invitations to the various campsites for an evening meal with me as guest. In return I was expected, after the meal to talk and then teach the troop a new camp fire song. These songs became popular and I persuaded Uncle Joe to make a book of songs I knew and have it duplicated so I could pass it out to the boys.

During my stay, my pioneering background led me to build two bridges on the camp. The first one was forty two feet long and crossed a gully which led to the canteen. The second was much more ambitious and crossed a river. This was a suspension bridge spanning some sixty five feet and I called this London Bridge.

I was able to accept many invitations to attend parties. Often they would be called Clam Bakes and I was invited to meet many people who were all interested in life in England.

One night every week all the camps would gather together around one huge bonfire and sing songs and perform sketches to the delight of all the other groups. During the evening there would be what was called a tapping out ceremony. All would sit facing the fire in total silence whilst someone would walk around behind them and tap them on the shoulder. These boys were selected for there leadership or prowess at the camp. They were to be made into real Indians of a tribe, the 'Order of the Arrow'.

I was selected at such an evening. All those selected were blindfolded and walked with one hand on the shoulder of the person in front up the nearby mountain. At various points each boy would be dropped off and left with just a blanket, on his own for the night. It was all a bit spooky and I am sure quite an ordeal for some of the younger boys.

The next day you had to serve your brother scouts all day and were not permitted to talk for twenty four hours. In this way I became a real North American Indian. I was presented with all the regalia, which I still proudly possess.

Often on my days off duty Uncle Joe would take us to see many places of interest. On the trip to the Potomac River we visited the scout camp at Lillie Aaron Straus. It must be one of the largest scout camps in the world - I am led to believe that it takes two days to cross it on horseback. Here I experienced the thrill of canoeing along one of the Country's best known rivers.

Before I left I went to the Rotary Club of Bel Air with Uncle Joe where I gave a talk on the life of Baden Powell and led the members in a sing song using the camp

My arrival at Broadcreek campsite Whiteford, Maryland,USA in 1963.

Service Above Self

ROTARY INTERNATIONAL

May it be known that

Raymond Maddock

was the Guest Speaker at the

Rotary Club of

Bel Air, Md. U.S.A.

and as an Expression of Appreciation for Courtesies extended to this Club we hereby present this Certificate,

Joseph Umbarger
SECRETARY

[illegible]
PRESIDENT

My much prized certificate from Bel Air Rotary Club in 1963.

fire songs from my book. I was given a certificate to commemorate the event.

Once the camp life had ended I met up with all the other students in that area. We were to go on a sixteen day trip by Greyhound bus along the eastern seaboard, and I was appointed leader of a group of 12 students

Before we departed we had a few days in Washington staying at the Stratford Hotel on East 23 Street. We visited the Pentagon and the White House. The last visit took us out to see Mount Vernon, the home of George Washington and the Arlington Cemetery. The day we were there, 28th August 1963, 250,000 negroes marched on the Capitol in a civil rights protest. It was an awe inspiring event and a day in the history of the world.

The coach took us on to Warsaw and then to Buffalo where we stayed with private families. We travelled on to Niagara Falls and into Canada just so we could all get our passports stamped.

On our arrival back in New York we were housed at the Great Northern Hotel to await the sailing of our boat back to England. I managed to find the time to go to the top of the Empire State building and on the 11th September sat in on a debate at the United Nations building, on Southern Rhodesia.

All too soon our tour was over. We set sail for home at the end of a wonderful summer. The boat was a Dutch ship called Groot Beer - great bear. On the homeward journey, I took on the job of editing the ships daily newspaper.

The last night's meal on the Groot Beer.

FAREWELL DINNER
Commander J.A.J. Reedijk.
Salad America
Iced Table Celery with Green and Ripe Olives
Consomme Madrilene
Poached Fillets of Haddock Hollandaise
Buttered Carrots - Boiled Potatoes
Roast Young Turkey - Cranberry Sauce
Straw Potatoes
Combination Salad
Egg Dressing
Dinner Rolls - Butter
Farewell Cake
Coffee

From the year of 1959 I printed an annual report on St. John's activities for eight years. I produced three Gang Shows, one pantomime and, combined with the

Patterson School of Dancing, two other stage spectaculars. Some of these shows were held at the Morton Jubilee Hall on Union Road, the social club of the Hovis factory given to the town by a Mr Morton.

The troop also had a most successful drum and bugle band. We always considered that we were the best even though it may not always have been the truth. We did however dominate the competition for the silver bugle most years. Graham Lockett and my brother Kenneth won it most years that I can recall and after a while it was no longer competed for.

Every year the band took on engagements such as church walks and playing the last post at Remembrance Day services. We also did other jobs like rose queen fetes in places like Knutsford and Middlewich. The band had to pay its way and looking through the reports it would appear that we would take on around sixteen engagements annually.

There were of course many social events some of which included the Guides. We held dances, Halloween's, tramps balls, and in 1959 a series of talent shows. Stuart Thompson playing his guitar won and went on to greater success with his own group. You may know him from his most successful car accessory shop on Park Lane.

Every year the troop took part in Bob-a-job week to raise funds for the headquarters in London - although if very successful the surplus went to our own troop. Later it had a title change as the minimum charge rose to be one pound in line with inflation.

At St. John's we had a good source of firewood in the form of off cuts from a large timber works in Manchester. We would collect the off cuts and split them into sticks and bundle them up and distribute them free as firelighters. Most houses still had open fires at the time.

Over the years we also had a very good parents' committee who raised funds for the group. In the year 1965/66, we managed to purchase the old school, now called Mafeking Hall, for £1,250. It gave the group much needed independence. It would no longer depend on the Church for a place to meet. This was important to me as many of our scouts were Methodists, Baptist and other religions. Once we gained that independence I came to the conclusion that we might operate more efficiently as an open group - not tied to any one church.

When I started with the group the vicar was a nice old gentleman called Robinson often referred to as Robbo. On scout nights he would often call at the Prince Albert in Newton Street and then come to read the closing prayers at the end of our meeting. When he retired he was replaced by the Reverend W. Lakeland. In his first year he dismissed the whole of the church choir over a dispute. He changed the services, to which the congregation had come accustomed, which led to many leaving the flock.

His attitude also contributed to the departure of our group scoutmaster Mr

The cast of one of our gang shows at St. John's. Includes Brian Haley, Geoffrey Sherratt, David Potts, Brian Smith, David Foden, Mr. Kwiatkovski, Brian Rose, Norman Oldfield, Derek Smith, Philip Morton, Raymond Henry, David Smith, Graham Wilson and Paul Band.

The cast of a Winter spectacular given at the Morton Jubilee Hall when the scouts teamed up with the Patterson dancing school with Glenda Harding, Diane Hehir, Derek Smith, Brian Smith, Philip Morton and the Malkin twins.

Whittaker. At the time I was the most junior member of the parochial church council and at an important meeting of the council the vicar announced that the church needed £7,500 to repair it, but an alternative was to spend £25,000 on the building of a new church on Weston Estate. I was the only member of the council to vote against this major move.

As a result the old church was demolished and we had this bright new church built on Earlsway. We now know it only lasted a few years and has now been knocked down and replaced. The result of the church being moved meant that due to distance the troop could now no longer parade with the band to church once a month. In fact the new church was further away than any other church in the town with a scout group, including Hurdsfield.

My idea of an open group grew stronger and I felt now was the time. My idea did not find favour with the vicar and whilst I was away in Europe he had me suspended from my position as scoutmaster under regulation 77(ii). When the new church was consecrated there was no place for any of the scouts. We were allowed to parade outside and raise the union flag but there were to be no seats within the church for any of the boys. We stood outside and watched all the bigwigs enjoy the service of dedication.

The outcome of a long drawn-out dispute was that I was dismissed as leader after eleven and a half years dedicated service. This was immediately followed by the resignation of ASM Howard Torson, Cub instructors Derek and Brian Smith, four members of the parents' committee and the disbanding of both the rover and senior sections of the group. Then followed the dismissal of troop leaders Graham Wilson and Phillip Morton who were both loyal members of the group.

The District Commissioner Harry Pleeth - *"Mr Maddock is one of the best scouters in the association"*, ADC Mr George Rathbone - *"Mr Maddock is a most trustworthy and efficient scout"*, and ADC Mr Stanley Albinson - *"Mr Maddock is a first class scouter and is doing a good job at St. John's"* all backed me with very kind words. But the vicar had the power to have me dismissed and gave no consideration to the damage it would cause to the scout movement in Macclesfield. I have no regrets for standing up to a pompous self-opinionated vicar, the most unchristian Christian I have ever had the misfortune to meet, but it led me to cease being an active scout in an association that I loved. I still fully support the aims of the movement today.

St John's Scout Band prior to a parade. Back row: Clifford Royal, Bob Isherwood, Michael Fytton, Trevor Davies, David Gidman, Jim Rose, ?.
Those seated Geoffrey Sherratt, ?, ?, Kenneth Maddock, ?, Graham Lockett, Wilfred Burgess.

The scout band leading Hurdsfield Church on their annual parade around the parish.
The front row of drummers are Kenneth Maddock, Johnny Blackburn and Jim Rose.

The delivery of firewood to pensioners in December 1966.

Brian Miller cuts the birthday cake on the first birthday of St. John's watched by the Rev'd Robinson.
Also: Miss Hannon, Roy Barton, Brian Swindells, Trevor Davies, David Gidman & Wilfred Burgess.

Anne Dugdale on Fred and Raymond Maddock on Dusky following their success at Harrogate in the sixty mile Golden Horseshoe ride organised by the Daily Telegraph on the 3rd September 1966.

Annual prize-giving at Macclesfield & District Riding Club with showjumper Michael Whittaker.

HORSES

I do not know just what it was that first caused me to take an interest in horses, but there were three events in my early life which may have been a trigger. My visit to New Brighton as a child on holiday and a ride on a donkey at the seaside. Later, whilst still in short trousers, my employment with Mr Bowers on his milk round with his horse Major. The third and most likely influence came whilst I was a 'maturing' pupil at King's school and I developed a passion for girls with long hair who rode horses. I have no idea why. Was it the horse or the girl?

Shirley Powell of Henbury was the first I had a crush on but she never knew and I never told her. My passion led me to travel on my bike to the local agricultural shows, Poynton, Hazel Grove and Bramhall, and enjoyed every minute of these events. It may seem very sad but I just loved to watch these lovely young ladies with their ponies performing in the ring.

I recall that as Shirley grew older she owned a horse called Winston C which won many events in the show jumping ring. The same horse competed in national events often ridden by a famous show jumper, Shamus Hayes.

Later in my life I became a founder member of the Macclesfield Agricultural Society. They regularly held annual shows in the South Park under the chairmanship of ex mayor, Alderman Hidderley. The show secretary was Eric Oliver who was later editor of the Macclesfield Advertiser. The shows had two very wet years causing a financial problem which led to its demise. The problem was exacerbated by the Borough council's charges for the reinstatement of the park and the fact that we could not close the public right of way which had to be fenced off at great expense.

On my return from America, and whilst building up my driving school business, I took on part time work at the Macclesfield Golf Club. The Burgess brothers took me on as a part time greenkeeper. I cut the grass, caught the moles, built new tees and greens, and generally improved the course. Whilst I worked there, up Hollins Road, I became acquainted with the riding school opposite the club. This was run by two girls Anne and Pat Dugdale, and their mother became a good friend to me. Anne ran the stables and she gave me riding lessons in exchange for doing jobs around the yard. It was an all female environment as their father, who had been Medical Officer of Health to Macclesfield Borough Council, had left to take up a post in Australia.

It rekindled my interest in horses - and girls. I can well remember Kathryn, Roberta, and the senior stable girl Jane McKinstry. She was a very keen rider and when she left school she took a job as a veterinary nurse with Wright and Morton. Jane's father was goalkeeper for Macclesfield Town football club.

As my interest in horses increased I elected to join a riding club - the East

Cheshire Combined Training Group. Anne was a member. The club had been formed by Wendy Ashton, Margaret Casson, and Iris Diamond and held its first meeting in 1962. I joined in 1965.

There was already a Macclesfield Riding Club and a Cheshire Equestrian Club. In 1965 I was to join the committee and help take the club to great success in the world of equestrianism.

I was attracted to the idea of long distance riding. In 1966 I competed in three such events. On each occasion I rode the pony I had learnt to ride on at the Dugdale stables and I was joined on each ride by Anne herself. The horse I rode was called Dusky although its full title was Naughty Nights.

The first of these events at Dalton Park, Beverley near Hull, was organised by the White Rose Riding Club. I borrowed a cow trailer from Henry Pass of Barracks Lane to transport my mount. Following the success of the first long ride we entered a qualifying 40 mile ride at Bainbridge in Yorkshire which was billed as 'The Fell and Pennine Ride'. On this occasion Anne and I travelled in a borrowed horse box. We both successfully completed the ride and qualified to enter the Sunday Telegraph 60 mile ride later that year. This major event on 3rd September 1966 started from the Great Yorkshire showground at Harrogate. I bought my first pair of jodhpurs so that I could look as though I knew what I was doing.

On the big day we were all set off in small groups at intervals of ten minutes. The first obstacle was the river. The river was so deep that I had to ride with my feet up onto the saddle in order to keep my feet dry. At the 40 mile post we were all inspected by the vet and many horses had to drop out at this point, but Anne and I were fit to continue. At that time I was extremely fit and my plan was to keep the horse fit by getting off and walking when the route was uphill, and getting off and running when the route was downhill. I covered about fifteen miles of the course on foot which was within the rules.

We were well organised with a working party which met us at various points on the route to clean and change the tack on both of our horses. Those in that team were Graham Wilson and Philip Morton and I think Jane also took part. They were a very skilled slick team.

We both completed the course in the time of ten hours and four minutes at an average speed of six miles per hour. We were presented with our bronze horseshoes and mine still has a place of honour in my trophy cabinet.

It was time to buy a horse of my own. I went with Anne to a dealer called Ray Almond who had stables at Madeley near Keele and I took a mare out for a test ride. This mare was a working hunter called Caramel and I was so impressed I agreed to buy and paid £180 including delivery to Macclesfield. To begin with the mare was kept at the riding school and earned her keep by my taking out some of the rides. When I moved up to Windmill Street in 1968 I got a field of my own and with the new house having a stable I was able to keep my horse at home. Over the next few years I was to own several horses.

In the years between 1967 and 1972 I organised on behalf of the ECCTG five very successful long distance rides. The first of those rides was held in May 1967 on a modest scale and started from Ridge Hill in Macclesfield, the home of Richard May. The course was over 25 miles of country with which I was very familiar. The ride covered Lamaload Reservoir, Jenkin Chapel, Charles Head Rainow, Bollington and Kettleshulme. We had 32 horses entered over three classes and the overall cup went to a Miss Cussons from Warrington whilst the other classes were won by Miss P. Harrison of Gawsworth and Anne Dugdale on Fred.

My second attempt was in May 1968 and started from Capesthorne Hall by kind permission of Lt. Col. Sir Walter Bromley Davenport MP. This ride had two classes, a 25 mile and a 40 mile route, with the first five home on the 40 mile ride qualifying for entry into the Sunday Telegraph Golden Horseshoe ride later that year. The winner on the day was Mrs B. Sheppard on her horse Pepino who came from Shrewsbury. The best placed junior entry was Susan Diamond on her horse Sweet Briar.

In May 1969 we had a 25 mile ride from the Robin Hood car park at Rushton with 29 riders. The winner on this occasion was Wendy Ashton. The fastest horse on the day covered the cross country route at an average speed of 6.8 miles per hour.

The following two rides both started from Swythamley Hall Park, the home of Lt. Col. Sir Philip Brocklehurst. The first, May 1970, covered 21 miles and included travelling across the top of the Roches. We returned to Swythamley in May 1972 for the last of the long rides. This time the course was only thirteen and a half miles but it thrilled the 32 riders who took part over this rough terrain. Alas, the days of the long rides were over.

I was most grateful for the assistance given by Sir Philip who was well into his old age at the time. He still owned a horse but I suspect he did not ride very often, if at all. I understand that he bred and trained his own mount when he entered as a private individual in the 1936 Olympic Games. He was knighted I believe for his part in the expedition to the south pole with the Shackleton party. I was very privileged to be shown around his private museum up at the hall where his trophies were on the wall, polar bears, penguins and other memorabilia.

During my membership of the ECCTG I was appointed as the bridle paths officer for mid and east Cheshire to the British Horse Society, and I surveyed all the bridle paths in my area. As a token of gratitude for my work within the club I was awarded a scholarship to spend a residential week at the Aughton Green Riding School. The school was run by Dorothy Johnson, a British representative at dressage on a number of occasions. I was allowed to take my own horse and although it was hard work at the time, it did improve my riding.

I served on the committee of the ECCTG for six years. In 1979 I left to join the

Macclesfield and District Riding Club - the rule was you could only be in one club. I became President and held the post until August 1987.

I would like to tell you about some of my horses now. At this time, as the number of days I rode out on my horse dwindled I came to the decision to breed a foal from my mare before she was too old. I took Caramel to Miss Margaret Paskin who ran the Sovereign Stud in Mobberley where she was covered by a champion palomino stallion called Palais de Danse.

The foal arrived just a few days late and coincided with the first moon landing on the 23rd May 1969. That space craft was called Snoopy and so that was the name I gave to the beautiful filly foal. She stayed with me as a faithful friend for the whole of her life, and was buried at Mecca in March 1995 having given me twenty eight years of extreme pleasure.

I returned Caramel to the same stud and in the May 1970 she produced a second foal which I christened Laredo. This colt foal was later to be sold to a blacksmith's daughter in Doncaster.

Now I received information about a mare in foal which was seriously neglected and starving. I contacted the owner and persuaded him to sell me the horse as I suspected it would die when foaling if not rescued. I loaded the mare, called Alice, into a horse box in a snow storm just hours before the road was blocked by snow. She produced her foal in May 1981. Alice was later sold to a young girl but kept at my stables. When the girl took up full time employment as a nurse I took the horse back.

I was also given as a free gift a little steel-grey stallion called Cheeky (Tovy Diplomat). The owner, who lived alone near Hanging Gate, Higher Sutton, had to go into hospital and did not expect to return. Cheeky was a real handful and I had to have him gelded. I do not recall just who I sold him to but I kept him for a long time.

My horse Snoopy was registered with the Palomino Society and over many years gave me great pleasure in the various competitions at novice level. In May 1973 Snoopy gave birth to a colt foal having been sent to the Sovereign stud. This foal I called Peanuts and it was eventually sold to a member of the Macclesfield Riding club, the daughter of a couple who were later to become committee members.

In May 1974 there was a second foal for Snoopy, a colt called Boots. Snoopy eventually, after twenty eight years of loyal service as a companion, was suffering and I had to let her go in March 1995. I put up a monument to her which I hope will be there long after I am forgotten.

At Ecolodge in Windmill Street I had stabling for up to six horses and over the years I had a number of different tenants. Two of these stayed with me for many years with different horses. One was Gillian Varty, the other was Susan Hammond. I knew Susan from her days at the High School and I went to her wedding. When I moved to Mecca her horses came too. When Snoopy went and I gave up horses altogether, Susan was able to find land of her own and erect stabling for her many horses.

The Riding Club Equitation Class on the field opposite Star Lane, with the football club in the background.

Nicola Pioli, daughter of the club's secretary.

Show jumping at the riding club with Dawn Hayter.

Pop Proctor, show jumping judge, hands out the rosettes.

Riding club field day, Raymond Maddock, Sir Nicholas Winterton and Margaret Ollier.

Rachael Bayliss signs autographs for Riding club members.

Kirsty Hamilton judges a fence on the cross country.

Macclesfield Riding Club fancy dress competition.

Below: Sue Honey accepts the trophy for winning the team jumping competition.

At the Macclesfield and District Riding Club, almost all the other members of the committee had children in the club so I was alone in being independent and unbiased. A close neighbour, Terry Wood, was elected to the position of Chairman and for many years we worked in close harmony to improve the running of the club until 1984 when he felt he had done enough and Keith Hamilton took over. Keith and I became good friends and worked together well. Over the years we worked together the capital assets and the standard of competition was improved.

The riding club's fund-raising event, a donkey derby.

During my eight years as president the land we had used for shows, opposite the Star Inn on London Road, was withdrawn and the club had nowhere to go. After a year of temporary land up Ridge Hill I purchased Mecca so the club would be able to continue. Everything went well until Keith decided it was time for him to leave. A new chairman and committee members arrived and we could not work together. In the end I had to ask them to leave Mecca and find an alternative site. It led to my resignation - in the best interest of the club I felt it was time to go. This was August 1987 and the club moved to premises in Bollington.

I had been successful in attracting a number of celebrities to our annual prize giving evening: Rachel Bayliss was a member of the British one day event team, and the biggest coup was the night when Michael Whittaker came to present the trophies. I always had a strong team of committee members. In addition to my two loyal chairmen there were Geoff Pickering, his wife and two daughters, John Hall, Sue Honey, Margaret Pass, Angela Eardley, Mrs Grimshaw, Mrs Brimelow, Mr and Mrs Rostron, and Mr and Mrs Bailey. There were others as well but my memory fails me and I apologise for any omissions.

During my presidency Mrs Simpson started a group of Riding for the Disabled at the Dugdale Riding School now operating from Blakelow Farm. Geoff Pickering and I joined her in the venture and I was later elected as chairman of the group in October 1980. One horse show I organised was held on the land of John Richards of Gawsworth Hall and the leading attraction was Red Rum, who won the Grand National more than once. I resigned as Chairman of the RDA in November 1986 when we had an influx of new members keen to make their mark - I left them to get on with the good work which Mrs Simpson had started.

Over the years I have also enjoyed the company of dogs, and besides my horse there are two dogs buried and remembered at Mecca. I purchased my first pup from a farm in Marple in 1978, a border collie which turned out to be a cross Alsatian. I called him Wolfie Smith - I saw no reason why a dog should not have both a Christian and surname. After twelve and a half years Wolfie met a sad end and was buried here at Mecca.

I still needed a dog to handle the sheep so I scanned the newspapers and found another one, again in Marple. I called him Lucky Limewell after his champion sire Limewell Blake. This time I had bought a pure bred Welsh border collie and he was a brilliant sheepdog, and most intelligent. As he grew older he started to go blind and could no longer do his job so I thought I would buy him a little helper. I found a local farmer with pups for sale and I picked out the one with the biggest feet, as I was told that big feet was a good sign in a dog. I called him Compo Symonite after *Last of the Summer Wine.*

In 2001 Lucky died peacefully and is buried at Mecca. He was a first class working dog and will not be forgotten. Now Compo is the boss and whilst he is not as good, he is a most affectionate dog, a first class mate and better than a wife - he does as he is told without question.

My dogs Lucky and Compo in 2000.

Compo Symonite shows off his badly cut front paw.

King's School class taken by one G.B. Mills. Those in the picture in no particular order were: Bowyer, Bateson, Wild, Unwin, Oldham, Lopez, Brough, Parrott, Leach, Millar, Dearden, Taylor, Clarke, McGrath, Hirst, Leigh, Lawrence, Davenport, Hunter, Webb, Donnelly, Munro, Gaskell, Mills, Wood, Mercer, Hopley and Maddock.

T.T. Shaw, headmaster at King's school, caught eating an ice cream cone at the high school fete.

King's School today.

HIKING & TRAVEL

When I started at the King's School walking became rambling and then serious hiking. I joined the school rambling club and I had the pleasure of exploring the various geographical features close to my home town. These weekend trips created a good deal of camaraderie.

THE KING'S SCHOOL YEARS - MACCLESFIELD EXPRESS

A master I owe the most to was Mr Burt who taught me English literature. I did not like English literature but this six foot plus man organised the rambling club. Most weekends in the summer he would organise a hike for the sixth formers, but myself, Keith Bradley and Howard Collier from the lower fourth, would regularly gate-crash the outings. As a result over the years I walked just about every footpath within ten miles of Macclesfield. Three things stick in my mind. One, we three fourth formers always walked well ahead of the main party. Two, our longest single hike was over a distance of 38 miles and we enjoyed every mile of it. The third and most vivid memory was that Mr Burt and the sixth formers always joked about the fact that in my packed lunch I always had a tin of rhubarb. I do not know why but I always did. I never knew why the others thought it so funny.

When I got my beloved bike it allowed me to travel freely over much greater distances, sometimes over one hundred miles in a day. I began to explore my county and soon other counties. A ride to Rhyl for the weekend was not unusual, and a ride of 138 miles in a day did not seem excessive at the time.

WEEKENDS - EXTRACT MACCLESFIELD EXPRESS

In the early 1950s, with money from my paper round, I achieved my goal of purchasing my own bicycle. This was no ordinary bicycle but a Super Lenten in electric blue with twenty seven inch wheels and not the usual twenty six inch. It had a light weight frame and GB alloy brakes. I was so proud of this machine that I would spend hours stripping it down and even polishing the ball bearings and replacing them with fresh grease. It was a labour of love. When you have to earn the money to buy a bike you usually look after it.

Every opportunity was taken to ride the bike and on one Saturday morning, along with friends David Marsden and Robert Lockett, we set out up Hurdsfield Road, passing the church at eight in the morning and arrived at Sheffield Railway station where we stopped for lunch. After lunch we rode south and arrived at a café in Ashby-de-La-Zouch for tea. We returned home via Derby and Ashbourne to arrive tired but happy at 10.15 pm.

Even more ambitious were our trips to Rhyl for the weekend. We would leave home after school on the Friday night and ride the 72 miles to Rhyl where we would make our HQ in an old railway wagon which was stuffed with old railway time tables and parked in a siding along side the River Clywd. After a fish and chip supper we settled down to sleep. At first light we would have a quick splash in the sea and then once again mount our steeds and make for Bangor or Anglesey. After a day's exploring we were glad to return to the old railway wagon. After a short rest we would leave our cycles and spend the evening at the fun fair in Rhyl finishing with the usual fish and chip supper before a good night's sleep.

On the Sunday morning we would start for home. We would each choose a different route, split up and travel as fast as possible to see who could make it home first. Cycle racing on the roads in the early fifties did not seem unusual but I suppose today it would be suicidal.

The next stage was to join the Youth Hostel Association which gave me even more scope for travel. My most ambitious trip was when I agreed to take my brother Kenneth onto the continent to further his education.

The trip did not start well as we stood on London Road, Lyme Green with our rucksacks trying to thumb a lift to Dover. By the end of that first day we had only got as far as Leicester where we booked in at a B and B for the night. The next morning we decided to travel by train down to Dover.

On the continent our first night in a French hostel was not encouraging. We were on camp beds in a loft at a farm, and the blankets were damp, the whole place smelt musty. However once we got to Lille we were in good spirits, the weather was good and the lifts were regular.

One of the best hostels we stayed at was in Köln in Germany on the banks of the Rhine. As we were booking in, a boy from Hyde near Manchester came up behind me and slapped me on the back as a greeting. Only a few weeks before that same boy had won the first prize in a lottery held at my scout troop.

We had a plan to visit my eldest sister who was stationed in Germany with her husband, an RAF officer. I had looked up the name of the station in an atlas and made a note of the map co-ordinates. But where I had expected to find my sister, the place was nowhere to be found. I enquired at a police station, who kindly looked up the town, only to find we were over one hundred miles from our planned destination.

We got to my sisters and spent two days in the married quarter and purchased a few bottles of duty free whisky when we left. We booked on a train which took us into Holland past miles and miles of tulip fields. When we arrived it appeared we were on the wrong train. Two trains left the station - we had paid for the slow train and we travelled on the fast one. But the guard was most understanding and let us off the surcharge. Would it happen today?

I was surprised at the standard of English spoken by the Dutch and their appreciation of what we had done for them in the war. We managed to visit the bridge at Remagen, the war cemetery at Arnhem, and the bulb fields around Harlem. When we finally reached Amsterdam, we entered a hostel on one of the canals to book in but there was a notice in English to the effect that no alcohol was permitted on the premises and just at that moment my brother put his rucksack on the stone floor and one of the bottles of whisky broke. We made a quick retreat only later to find his sleeping bag well and truly soaked with the offending liquid.

There were more places to see when I started as a coach operator and went into horseriding. A weekend at Badminton Horse Trials in Gloucestershire, and a week's stay at the Horse of the Year Show at Wembley.

Most of my earlier coach trips involved schools and a regular customer was the Macclesfield High School for Girls. One of my first trips was a tour down south taking in St Albans, Stonehenge, Maiden Castle, and the Avebury stone circle. The following year I took a party to Hadrian's Wall and all the Roman forts from Walls End to Bowness on Solway. In fact I got so knowledgeable about the wall after several tours that I was often encouraged by the teachers to lecture the pupils myself.

Another regular haunt was the Marquis of Anglesey's castle where I have spent many enjoyable weeks with school parties. The castle was for a short time used as a 'training ship' but later used by the Cheshire Education authority as an outward bound centre. I had a wonderful week with a school party at a field centre at Colwyn Bay in 1974.

Probably the best series of tours were those organised by Derek Brumhead a lecturer in Geology at the College of Further Education in Manchester. The first was a week in July 1970, when we stayed at a field centre at Slapton in Devon. They were a friendly bunch of students of all ages. The following year was based in Anglesey, then in 1972 I undertook the longest of these tours to the Isle of Skye where we stayed at a small hotel in Portree. I had a most wonderful time - the work was a holiday for which I was being well paid.

In July 1973 we spent a week at a field centre at Pembroke Dock. Despite its name it is a country mansion set in beautiful countryside and most peaceful. I quite got into the swing of things and my knowledge of geology improved significantly. The next two years were spent in Northumberland where our base was Alnwick castle. The other half of the castle was occupied by the Percy family - the Hotspurs of Wars of the Roses' days. We got as far as Durham Cathedral, Banburgh Castle and Lindisfarne. My most vivid memory is the drive up from the beach at Robin Hoods Bay, the steepest hill that I have ever driven up with a coach. I had my doubts at times whether we would reach the top.

The last two of these tours was with a new coach based on a Mercedes chassis and built for me at Formby in Lancashire. In 1973 I entered it in the National Coach

Rally at Blackpool which started from Wigan. My navigator and time-keeper was Steven Cleworth who had been a pupil of mine when I was teaching driving. We were very successful and I came away with a cup for the Concorde d' Elegance class which I still proudly keep in my trophy cabinet.

Apart from the scouts, I did a number of very enjoyable tours on the continent, most of them travelling in a twelve seater safari Landrover but some with a minibus. I think that I have actually driven in fifty five countries of the world - that still leaves a few to go and my travelling days are over. I have never travelled on a package holiday or flown by air so I like to think that as far as possible my travel was environmentally friendly.

The longest trip I ever undertook was with both a Landrover and a mini bus driven by my old troop leader Graham Wilson, and with Pat Dugdale. It took us all the way overland to Turkey. The trip lasted twenty one days and only cost the passengers twenty three pounds each. That included all the food and camping equipment. The object of the trip was to follow in the footsteps of St.Paul and the ancient history of the area was most fascinating. On the return journey coming through Yugoslavia, the engine on the minibus blew up and I had to tow it into Belgrade. It could not be fixed so half the party were sent home by train and the vehicle was later repatriated by the AA.

There were many other trips, like Italy and Greece. I did however make two trips which were not for profit. In 1973 I took some friends on a tour of the Loire Valley just to see the castles and sample the region's food. This was the last actual holiday that I ever took.

I did of course visit many sites of interest in England with my coach business. I visited many theatres with school parties and on each occasion I would see the performance. I have watched a lot of Shakespeare in my time! There were trips to gardens, and to museums, to cathedrals, battlefields, and many other places which added to my education.

As a member of the Country Landowners Association, I also attended many places of interest: Rolls Royce in Crewe, JCB in Rocester, the Ellesmere Boat Museum, the home of the Duke of Westminster near Chester. My minibus also transported the staff and actors of Granada when I covered a number of programmes made in my area in 1973. I have enjoyed travel as much as any other part of my life, and it certainly does broaden the mind.

FRIENDS

I can only recall a few friends in my class at Athey Street school in the early 1940s. There was Cyril Pratt, a red-headed boy who lived at a chip shop in Newton Street, near to the Prince Albert pub. A very big lad was called Brian Frame and a much smaller boy, Ernest Webb. The only girl I recall was Vera Bramwell. At the early age of eight, I wrote a letter to her at her home address in Armitt Street. Her response the next day at school was daunting and it put me off girls for many years to come.

I had a lot of good mates in Barton Street, 'our gang', even though I was the only one to attend a grammar school.

OUR GANG EXTRACT MACCLESFIELD EXPRESS MAY 1994

At the age of eleven I moved to a house in Park Lane, which at that time had doctors' surgeries on both sides - so we were never troubled by neighbours. Our back garden came out onto Barton Street where all my friends lived. This was in the late forties when Barton Street was still cobbled and had no parked cars.

The natural leader of the gang was Robert Lockett, from 27, whose mother was Welsh and whose father worked on the railway, repairing wagons. He had a younger brother Graham. Next door to him at number 29 lived Gordon Lennard, a little older and as such not a full member of our gang. John Hough from number 17 had a younger sister . He later went on to become a first class football referee. I recall playing alongside him for St. Andrews.

At number 1 lived Roland Smith who later became the landlord of the Three Pigeons in Little Street. I vividly recall having our annual bonfire in his back yard. When the fire was lit a very large rat ran out of the fire and later we had to dowse the fire with water when it threatened to set fire to the houses.

At number 19 lived David Ashness, who later worked for the GPO and had two sisters, Joan and Marion. All the three had bright red hair. There was also Graham Jones and Geoffrey Evans. The member who later became my best friend for years, lived in a house which had doors onto both South Park Road and Armitt Street. That was Roy Barton who went on to work for the gas board. He later moved into his aunt's old house in Hatton Street.

At the time we often played football or cricket in the street and only stopped when Mr Bowers passed with his horse and float, or an irate resident could not stand the noise. It was a period when all the older female residents would compete to see who could keep the cleanest step and footpath in front of their house. They would regularly be seen swilling the flags and then taking a donkey stone to the step. Some would perform the act weekly but the most enthusiastic did it daily.

At the bottom end of the street was Lennard's newsagent and on the opposite corner, Mrs Place's shop where one could buy anything from paraffin and firelighters, to potatoes or gas mantles. At the other end of the street was a grocer's shop where we purchased our daily bread and on the opposite corner was Mr Kirk's. He was a photographer and he lived with his sister. He used to go out on an old motorcycle to all the outlying schools to photograph the pupils. His prints were always done in sepia.

At that age, Gorton and Kellett the monumental masons held a special interest for me. Many was the time I sat and watched them chip away at a lump of marble to create a magnificent epitaph for a recently departed.

At the grammar school I was in a form of thirty three boys and I received an excellent education. But I was always in the bottom three in my class and left the school early by choice. I can recall the faces but not too many of their names. I do remember Jack Beck who later became a police sergeant and Peter Burgess, one of three Burgess's in my class, who was landlord of the Prince Albert pub for many years and whom I still bump into occasionally.

Probably the most memorable of my class mates was Geoffrey Rose who was my usual partner when playing truant. We often went to his house on Oxford Road as his parents were always out at work. Another classmate with whom I was very friendly was John Bateson. We spent a lot of time together at shows as he was an ardent rabbit fancier - he not only entered prize-winning rabbits but also helped judge at some of these shows.

Then there were the masters who influenced my life -

THE KINGS SCHOOL YEARS EXTRACT MACCLESFIELD EXPRESS

Although I had been very bright at Athey Street School my move to the Kings School came as a shock. Maybe I did not try enough but I always found myself competing for bottom place in the class with one David Bailey. This experience does not seem to have hampered either of our progresses in later life though.

As a new boy I remember T.T. Shaw, the headmaster, would frequently arrive at morning assembly wearing carpet slippers. The head boy was Dan Massey, a huge monster of a rugby player from Gawsworth. Nobby Clarke who taught us history. He still lives in Park Lane. Mr Harvey was deputy head and taught us French with little success. I was however very good at mathematics taught by Johnny Yeoman Rushbrook. I often wonder if you are good at a subject because you like it or you like a subject because you are good at it.

Two masters were special for me. One was Mr. Jardine who taught metalwork, and the other Mr Jones, who taught art, and whose wife taught at the Girls High School. I recall that he always referred to his pupils as bunny rabbits and when there was snow on the ground he would arrive at school on skis

I did not like school very much, I played truant too much and I could not wait to leave and start work. We were always told that school days are the happiest days of your life - I might have agreed if I had not had to spend so many of them at school.

There were good times though. I liked playing on 'the rock' at lunch time, our version of stone age cricket, using a stone for the ball and a tree branch for a bat. Then after school dinners we would go down the bottom of the playing field to catch the 1.10 pm train, The Comet, on its way to London (we were trainspotters then).

One thing always puzzled me about the Kings School. Whilst I was there they erected large wrought iron gates at the main entrance to commemorate the war. There was much pomp and ceremony which we all attended but from that day onward, we, the pupils, were not allowed to use those gates.

Over this period I was also in the scout movement. In addition to those scouts I have already mentioned I would like to add the following friends who come to mind. The following were all fellow scout leaders: George Foot and Gordon Stiles of Sutton St. James, Raymond Chadwick of Christ Church, Les Hutchinson of St Michael's, Richard Wright of 2nd Bollington, John Houghton of St Paul's, Derek Davenport of Hurdsfield, and my old classmate at Kings, Keith Parrott of Gawsworth.

Raymond Henry, Jimmy Genders, Graham Russell were other leaders in my troop, and Brian Miller, David Gidman, Barry Trueman, Howard Torson, Gordon Byron, Trevor Davis and Barry Swindells were all founder members of the troop.

Other boys I recall at St Johns were David Potts, Brian Haley, John and Geoffrey Sherratt, Roger and David Foden, Brian Smith, Derek and Alan Smith, David Smith, Paul Bamford, Brian Rose, John Ellis, Eric and Donald Malkin twins, Elvin Birch, Steven Ridgeway, Christopher Carbery, Stephen Murphy, Colin Wolstenholme, Harry

Royal, Roger Tyrie, Christopher Davenport, Paul Mackay, Norman Oldfield, Kerrian Rogers, John Whitney, John Costello, Dennis Clowes, John Muir, Ernest Webster, Alan Perry, and John Cooper. I do apologise if some names are not in this list.

One other friend, Keith Yearsley, was connected to St Johns but was not in the scouts. He was the choirmaster until the new vicar dismissed the choir. Despite this rebuke he went on to be a leading light in the town as a conductor of several well-known choirs and also became a headteacher.

When I was square bashing in Bridgnorth I met a boy from Northwich and we became good friends. Brian Capper and I still exchange Christmas cards.

At the age of about fifteen I started to take an interest in girls. Maybe I was a late starter - perhaps I had too many other interests. I have spent some time reading through my old diaries, which I kept from about 1955. In 1955 I met my first true love. Her name was Olive Massey and we used to meet in the South Park on a regular basis. We spent many happy hours in each others company. My diary recalls that on the 16th November 1956 I took Muriel Gould to the Majestic cinema, something of a coup at the time as I knew she always fancied Robin Dorey. I think I had a bit of an inferiority complex as far as girls were concerned. I courted a girl from Bollington called Gillian in 1957, a sort of long term relationship.

During my time as a wages clerk at Parkside my job each Thursday was to hand out the wage packets to the weekly paid. I was the junior of four staff with Albert Wrigley, boss, Geoffrey Bennett and Richard Hankinson. Our office was next to the front office, under the tower, near the enquiry office for all visitors. One other member of the office staff I remember well is Raymond Roach from whom I took over as treasurer of the social club.

The overall boss was Geoffrey Locke. The chief male nurse was Frank Willoughby. Sid Watmough was the full time fire officer and it was he who headed the Macclesfield Civil Defence of which I was a member. Then there was Roland Kershaw the printer who did lots of good work for me in his own time. A friend called Arthur Norbury was the farm manager. His brother Geoffrey also worked on the hospital farm where a large number of pigs were reared. When the farm closed down Geoffrey teamed up with another member of the staff, Kenneth Burgess, tinsmith, and they opened a business at Broken Cross selling and servicing lawn mowers. Now they both have separate businesses in the town run by their sons.

When I moved into the coach business I found a new circle of friends as my business expanded. The first was Roy McCarthy, whose son Andy now runs the firm, then Ron Leech and his son also entered the coach business. Later came Arthur Elkin who employed John Simpson as a mechanic and John inherited the business on the death of Arthur. There was also Warwick Marsh, Kenneth Hammond, and Hadyn Jones. Hadyn married an old friend of mine Mary Sutton from Hollins Road, and his son Gary took over from him when he retired and went to live in the Isle of Man.

I was later joined by George Brookfield of Stockport and Joe Keeling of Gawsworth whose wife Jean was a friend and member of the riding club. Another friend who came into the business was Roger Hill who later moved to Congleton.

I had a monopoly of school transport in the town. At the point of my retirement I was carrying some one thousand pupils a day to and from school in hired coaches. This brought me into contact with a large number of drivers who have remained friends, like Tony Sutton, Peter Thornicroft, and Mick Lomas. Malcolm Forster did not drive for me but it was as a result of the coach work that we became good friends.

I could not list all the members of both riding clubs but I would like to talk about some. Firstly there was Wendy Ashton, chairperson of the ECCTG and the daughter of an-ex mayor of the town, Councillor Hope from Upton Hall. I taught both her son and daughter to drive and became a good friend of the family, and I still see Philip from time to time. He owned the building firm of Ashton & Holmes at Sutton Sidings now run by Travis Perkins. Regrettably Wendy died as the result of a fall from a horse, she was always a rider who knew no fear, and it was a great loss to the club. I still have many fond memories of my visits for coffee at Swanscoe Hall.

As the president of the Macclesfield and District Riding Club I came into contact with hundreds of young riders all of whom I thought of as my children. I loved each and every one of them, they were all wonderful kids. But I cannot say that for all of their parents, many of whom were too ambitious for their offspring. I often had to mediate between irate parents over the result of a riding class.

Cheri Whittle came to Macclesfield from Bolton with her mother who had taken a job as housekeeper to a retired tax inspector. She brought with her a horse with which she had had a great deal of success back in Bolton. Cheri became a good friend, like a daughter to me and in 1986 I gave her the job of house-keeping when my Saturday girl left for full-time employment. At the age of sixteen Cheri became a model. A truly remarkable young girl I will never forget. Children like her made the job of President worth while - compensating for any problems with parents.

Many may wonder about my sexual orientation as I have never married. I never felt the urge to propose marriage although I did have three long term relationships. I am not afraid to admit that the first time that I had sexual intercourse was at the age of twenty six and then with a married women.

The first serious girlfriend I had was Mary Downing, the daughter of a local fire fighter. I was just seventeen at the time and driving for the first time. It lasted into my period of national service. I think we just drifted apart. My second relationship started during my period at Parkside hospital with a cadet nurse called Joan Mellor. We hit it off from the start and were together for two years. The next relationship was the best and lasted three years. Sandra Jones lived over a sweet shop lower down Park

Lane. I taught her to drive and she later acted in a little cine film I made about learning to drive. We shared many interests and attended the Brunswick Church and the youth club. She also helped in my activities with the scout movement. When I went to America as a camp councillor, she tried to persuade me not to go and although our friendship continued on my return, she eventually decided to end it. I was devastated. But life went on and I picked myself up. I think, like me, she never married and I often wondered if we might have made a good couple.

That was the last of my serious relationships but several years later I did have a friendship with a German au pair girl called Anne Meinken from Bremen. I was later to take two separate holidays at her parents home in Germany. We shared an interest in horses and she took on the work of looking after my horses - she had trained at a well-known riding establishment in Germany. She eventually fell in love with a soldier and left the town. It did not last long and she is now in America but on the two occasions she has been back to Macclesfield she has paid me a visit.

I suppose, all in all, friendship has always been more important to me than sex - and the lack of marriage perhaps has allowed me to do more, and to be a friend to more people. I hope so.

Young love. Mary Downing.

Sandra Jones. True love?

Joan Mellor

LAWS AND DISORDER

I want to talk about public officialdom, council officers, elected representatives, Macclesfield Borough Council, Cheshire County Council, the Police, and the Highway Authorities.

I feel sure that you all have come into contact with unreasonable officials, the 'jobsworth' boys. Most of you keep a stiff upper lip and never complain, but I am not like that, if I see an injustice I have to write about it. I keep notes and make my complaints official. Over the years I have written dozens of articles in the letters column of the local paper. I write on anything that effects me directly although I will take up the case of injustice of an individual if I think that I can make a difference.

I have been involved directly in nine public appeals over the last forty years - in most I have been successful. All these appeals cost you, the tax payer money, much of which was squandered needlessly by your local council.

Then there is the incompetence of your police force. We have all got tales of asking for police help and being ignored. The problem is that those in power do not listen to the public, they treat us like idiots. They seem to have the attitude that only they know what is good for us, from the top down, including the Prime Minister.

Some obvious subjects for scrutiny are Danegate, the return of the market to its rightful place, the lack of a cinema, the closure of Ryles Park School, the route of the Silk Road, and today the idea of building the Magistrates Court on the car park at Whalley Hayes.

Perhaps I could start with Danegate when the council lied to us in order to get their plans approved just because they owned half the land and other vested interests wanted it to go ahead, despite public opposition. We were told that two large companies would leave the town if the scheme did not go ahead. This did not happen. Later they failed to hold the developers to their responsibility to pay for a road bridge over the railway from the Lyme Green Business Park.

A campaign was started by Carl Massey and Vic Barlow against the development, supported by a large number of other interested bodies. I wrote six letters in 2001 and I would like to reproduce just one of these from the Macclesfield Express.

PIE IN THE SKY. COUNCILLORS HAVE PLUNGED US INTO DANEGATE MESS

So the Council are to press ahead with the Shepherds' application for Danegate on the grounds that it will create employment despite the rate in Macclesfield being well below the national average. There are more job vacancies than unemployed people in the town.

We were led to believe that Gradus and B & Q were already committed. It now seems that this is not the case. Just how much consideration has been given to the practicalities of bridging the railway and at what cost?

It is in the plan to ruin many of the wildlife habitats but they propose to create new ones. Where? On the contaminated ground which has been used for many years for scrap and car breaking. Is this just a smokescreen?

Do they really intend to build us a new football academy to the east of London Road as shown in the paper? In my opinion it is all just pie in the sky. What is the real plan? Could it be just an access road for an incinerator for when the tip finally closes? Now is the time for these questions to be addressed and not when councillors have voted to plunge us into this unwanted mess.

I am old enough to remember they used the same arguments for Scraggs at Langley which deprived the village of green fields and its cricket ground.

The Danegate proposal can only increase traffic on Congleton Road already tailing back to the Rising Sun in a morning. Will the new road create a rat run onto London Road itself already pushed beyond its capacity. Just say NO to Danegate.

Affluence in our society is much of the cause of our complacency, and the reliance on debt. England is one of the most populated countries in the world having 960 persons to the square mile compared with USA 72 and in Australia only six. We are more heavily populated than both India and China so our land needs to be carefully used and food production must come top of the list. We have the highest crime rate in the industrialised world, the largest number of teenage pregnancies in Europe and top the list in the abuse of drugs and alcohol

Someone once said, "For evil men to succeed it only requires that all good men do nothing". If you just sit back in front of the telly and say "It doesn't affect me" then one day you will wake up and find that it does. Wake up, and ask your councillor now where he or she stands and let's not be pushed around by big business telling us what we need. It is only what they want that motivates them.

In the end the council were pressured into holding their council meeting at the leisure centre so the public could attend in force. Cynically they picked the 5th November at 5 pm. How wrong they were. Around a thousand people turned out, and many of the councillors who had voted in favour of Danegate changed their vote under the eyes of the public.

Even this caning did not deter them as after only a few years they were back with Danegate 2. They now proposed a 'learning zone' which they thought the public might support. Again the public cited the problem with traffic. This scheme was even worse than the first one. I once again, like many others, wrote letters to the paper.

LEADER ACTING LIKE A DICTATOR

Last time we were told that at Danegate, B&Q and Gradus were committed to the development and would leave the town if the planning were refused. We were also told of a football academy and even possibly a cinema.

We were told that the developer would appeal the decision and sue the council for vast sums of money.

Now Councillor Burns is at it again. We are led to believe that if the new learning zone did not go on Danegate it could be lost to the town.

I'm all in favour of the zone at Ryles Park rather than more houses but if Councillor Burns is so keen on the zone, maybe it should go to Wilmslow - I suspect it would be a case of 'not in my backyard'.

Councillor Burns should remember he was elected to represent all the people and not just those in Wilmslow. He should stop acting like a petty dictator!

Has he already forgotten November 5th last year? Does he think he knows what is best for the people of our town? Has he forgotten the reasons for the opposition to Danegate then? The problems are still the same, increased traffic, poor ground, loss of natural habitat etc.

The sheer arrogance of the man! 'For God sake go and go now', we can manage our affairs without you. I will put my faith and support behind any councillor of any party who will speak for Maxonians and not for themselves.

Let us rid ourselves of these self-opinionated outsiders who want to take over our town. Give us back our market place and our old council.

I'm pleased to say that my wish was granted. Councillor Burns, following a lot of criticism in the press, finally departed the scene.

There are other poor decisions that have been made on our behalf:

The refusal to allow a cinema to be built at Lyme Green Business Park.

The change from industrial to retail of the same business park.

The premature closure of Ryles Park school.

Allowing Sainsburys to build a supermarket on the site of the town's infirmary and permitting them to close Prestbury Road.

The building of a town hall extension in a conservation area, and with a leaky roof.

The new Jordangate multi-storey car park in the wrong place for shoppers.

Putting a weight limit on Hulley Road which was built to service the industrial estate causing vehicles a two mile detour clogging up the roundabout at Tescos.

The ill fated blue badge parking scheme which they told us worked in other towns. Well it did not work here. Another waste of money.

The first attempt to pedestrianise Chestergate against advice, abandoned after only a few days on police advice.

The latest scandal - the new extension to the part time police station. I've seen better designed pig pens - a monstrosity in an area of conservation.

Another matter. An attempt was made to close Star Lane to through traffic. The parish council was not even informed of the plan even though it was in their parish. They only became aware when they read my letter to the paper:

The new town hall extension built with a leaky roof and now undergoing extensive refurbishment after only a few short years.

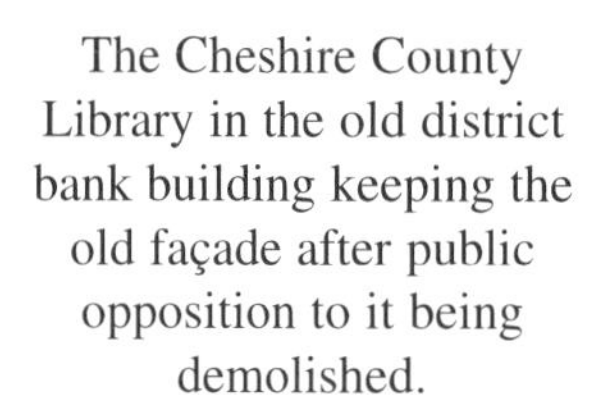

The Cheshire County Library in the old district bank building keeping the old façade after public opposition to it being demolished.

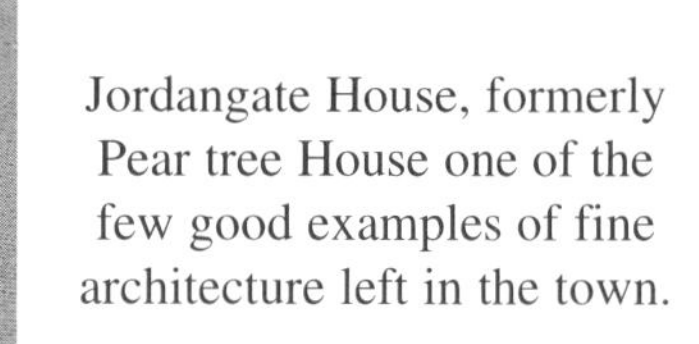

Jordangate House, formerly Pear tree House one of the few good examples of fine architecture left in the town.

Cotterills in the Market Square one of the few remaining old buildings left in the town brought up to date by Carl Massey a concerned Maxonian.

The new multi storey car park on Jordangate built in the wrong place and only suitable for small cars.

The new police station extension built in Brunswick Street 2005, a cheap and nasty example of poor architecture in a conservation area of the town.

The Lyme Green Industrial Estate, not in Lyme Green and no longer an industrial estate but a retail park.

STAR LANE CAR BAN COULD BE FOR EVER 20TH DECEMBER 1995

I wish to bring to the attention of the people of Macclesfield, that unless they act promptly they will be permanently prevented from driving along Star Lane. The department of transport is about to make an order that will close Star Lane to through traffic at a point where it crosses the railway line.

The reason for this appears to be a condition of planning approval by the Macclesfield Borough Council placed on an application made by Marston Thompson and Evershed PLC to enlarge the Star Inn and its car park. I have no objection to the proposed alterations but having seen the plans I can find no justification for the closure of Star Lane to traffic.

At present vehicles entering and leaving Moss Lane and going to and from the town centre use the busy and sometimes dangerous junction at the Moss Rose football ground. Those who use Moss Lane to get to and from Lyme Green, Sutton and the new retail park, use Star Lane. If it is closed, all that traffic will be forced to use the junction by the Moss Rose football ground. The potential for accidents with the large increase in right turning traffic is so enormous that it far outweighs any planning application for a pub car park extension.

In addition one might consider the implication for traffic on days when Macclesfield Town FC play at home. I wonder what the police have to say about that.

The closure was prevented, but we must all be vigilant as officials often like to do things with as little publicity as possible. Over the years I have written dozens of letters to the press about officialdom and to my memory only one in praise. This was for the opening of the Middlewood Way footpath. I was also fortunate to be given an invitation to the opening by the council, where I met David Bellamy.

One of the biggest blunders, although we have all got used to it now, was the decision to build the town 'bypass' through the middle of the town, cutting it in half.

TOWN CUT IN HALF - MACCLESFIELD EXPRESS 24TH JUNE 1992

Any day now we can expect the grand opening of the town bypass, the only one to cut a town in half. We will be greeted by hoards of officials in an orgy of self congratulation. They will all have forgotten that it was 54 years in the planning and four years in the construction and only one year late despite mild winters and no penalty clause.

The new road bears no resemblance to the plan put before the public at a meeting several years ago in the town hall. The final route which appears to have changed week by week no longer passes Arighi Bianchi's on stilts. Buxton Road is left open and Gas Road closed instead. It has bred a large number of roundabouts and traffic lights - not on the original plan. It now finishes, not with a roundabout at the bottom of Windmill Street, but traffic lights on the famous hump in Mill Lane. Perhaps this hump is to match the one at the other end, both products of bad planning.

The Star Inn, London Road, July 2005 about to be demolished to make way for another car showroom.

The Star Inn as it looked in 1939.

Bridge pillars in the wrong place having to be rebuilt, walls not coming into line, several claims for damage to adjoining properties and endless problems for the poor residents and businesses affected by the work.

No doubt we will be told how much better the traffic flows compared with the last few years of traffic chaos. No one will compare it with the period before it was planned. The truth is that after years of inconvenience we have been saddled with a white elephant at great expense which will not solve Macclesfield's traffic problem. It has just shuffled the pack, moving jams from one place to another. Those in Park Lane will now suffer at the expense of those in Oxford Road.

*We are now told that thousands are to be spent on another traffic survey to ascertain the needs of the town. Did they learn nothing from their previous blunders? Is it not time we consulted the people who use the roads? How much longer must we finance incompeten*ce?

Apart from the conflicts with the town hall which appear in earlier chapters I have been pursued relentlessly without any great deal of success on several occasions by their enforcement officers. They tried to stop me improving an access from London Road onto my property but I ignored them. When they did not follow up their threats I sent them a card on each anniversary to ask when they were going to force me to reinstate the old access. They did not respond. On more than one occasion they wrote to me telling me that I required planning approval for works I was carrying out. They were wrong, so again I ignored them.

I wonder if you know that you need planning approval to erect a flag pole outside your home, or to erect a fence more than two metres high. You do not however need planning approval to plant a hedge which may grow to more than two metres high. You need a tipping license to bring in or take out materials like soil to your property but you do not need permission to move soil around on your own property.

The council tried to stop me infilling my land in order to improve it. They even followed and stopped lorry drivers who were delivering to my land on the grounds that they were breaking the law. Rubbish. I told them where to get off.

Many people ask the advice of the planners. They are usually told to make a planning application, which costs you money, then they will decide if your application is necessary. Most people do not require planning approval to build an extension to their home and so long as it complies with the building regulations at the time you may well not even need to tell the town hall.

My home at Mecca was built in the green belt after going through the procedure of a full planning enquiry which upset the local planners. As a result, for a time after, they kept sending round enforcement officers to spy on what I was doing on the pretext that they had received information that I was carrying out works which required their approval. In the end I painted in letters, one foot high with yellow paint, NO PUBLIC OFFICIALS at the entrance to my property. This was picked up by the press and they wrote an article with a photograph in the Express 25th January 1995. This, along with the new gates and a camera at the entrance, has effectively stopped them.

Just to give you an example of how silly they can be, I wrote to the highways about an oak tree on my boundary with the highway. I considered it may in the future fall down in a storm and obstruct the highway. I suggested that I remove it in the interest of public safety, as I was planting over ten thousand trees at the time. I offered to pay for the felling but they put so many obstructions in the way that I decided to let it stand until it fell across the road and the council would have to remove it.

I established through the proper channels the right to have a house at Mecca. At the same time I am well aware that at least two councillors and one officer have had permission to build homes in the green belt in direct contravention of government guidelines - and if I was very cynical I might ask just how many officers have left the Council's planning department to work for P.R. Jones who seem to me to be the most favoured company when housing developments are approved in Macclesfield. I could write a lot more but it may well be considered as an accusation of corruption.

So much for the Town Hall. Now the policing of our town. We probably all have interesting stories to tell, most of them not very complimentary. Just occasionally we hear of where the outcome led to the conviction of a criminal. More often than not we hear of the failure of the police to secure a conviction. There are many reasons why they are so ineffective and most of these go back to government policies. They have been bound by rules, 'political correctness' and mountains of paperwork. They are expected to reach targets which affect their ability to do their work.

Police actions leading to a conviction in a court case represent only about 4% of all reported crimes. The crown prosecution service will only take a case to court if they feel they have an 80% chance of a conviction - and in the courts the police are often humiliated when magistrates hand down what in the eyes of the public seem to be derisory sentences. It must be most demoralising to keep arresting the same people for the same offences only to have the judiciary slap the offender on the wrist and tell them not to do it again. You only have to stand outside the Macclesfield Magistrates Court to see these yobs smoking, drinking, swearing, and boasting as to how their solicitor got them off with a sob story.

I must now give my views on a deteriorating service which I have kept records on over the last thirty years. The police take every opportunity to trumpet their successes on our television screens even allowing whole programmes to be made about them. They do not tell us about their failure to protect the public against problems most of us face nearly every day.

Here in Cheshire, every so often, we get a free newspaper telling us just what the police are doing for us. It may be on recycled paper, it may even be money well spent, but it often deceives the public in its detail. Their definition of the truth differs from mine. I read Your Policing - I expect that most of you just bin them without a second glance as propaganda.

One stated *"All reported crimes are investigated".* Well that is just not true. I think that you will find that around 75% of all reported crimes are just recorded and filed with no further action taken. They do not have the number of officers to investigate all reported crimes.

I have just been reading the 'Policing Plan 2005/06' which states that 400 experienced police officers respond to emergency calls and that if a burglar is still at the scene an officer will be sent straight away. This is not the case. On 19th March 2005 I telephoned the police to report a theft in progress and was told by one of these experienced police officers to *"sit tight, a patrol car will be with you shortly".* I am still waiting. I later found out that my call had been logged and that no further action was to be taken, I did not even get a phone call. The police may well be stretched to the limit but it does not help their cause to deceive the public into thinking that they are doing something when most of us know that they are not.

I am firmly of the opinion that nearly all the young men who apply to become police officers hope they will make a difference. Most pass out wanting to do the job but are held back by silly rules and regulations. And we appear to have a lot of older officers approaching their retirement who try to avoid work, happy to sit behind a desk so they do not get their hands dirty while they look forward to their pensions.

POLICE AVOID WORK AT ALL COSTS 8TH SEPTEMBER 2004

I recently had my property damaged by a vehicle which left the scene without stopping. As I had some details of the vehicle I thought that the police would be of some help, perhaps tell me who the owner or the driver was.

I telephoned the police station in Macclesfield and got a call centre (in India?) identifying themselves as Cheshire constabulary. I asked for the police station in Macclesfield and was transferred to another call centre.

I explained my problem and the lady kindly informed me that it was a civil matter and that I should contact a solicitor. I checked my facts and decided she was wrong, so called again only to find myself third in a queue for an operator. When I did get to speak to a person I was advised to go in person to the police station in Macclesfield and make an appointment to see a police officer.

I made the journey to the police station in Macclesfield and found three civilians manning the desk, not a police officer in sight. The three civilians were of no help, but they did tell me that I could make an appointment to see a police officer in three days time; that police officers do not make home visits any more and under the data protection act they would not be able to give me the details I was asking for.

So we have a police force which deflects calls to avoid working, does not do home visits and has a waiting time of three days to have an interview. I suspect that the claimed reduction in the number of reported crimes is because the public do not have a policeman to report it to. No wonder the criminals are having a field day.

One of the main stumbling blocks I feel is the career police officer who quickly rises through the ranks, probably with a university degree, who feels that he knows everything. He comes up with grand schemes, mostly to save money and not to reduce crime. Many of these schemes look good on paper but often do not work in practise. Having then made a cock up in one force, he moves on. We then have a different man with a very decorative hat but with very little under that hat.

REDUCE CRIME NOT STATISTICS 20TH MAY 1998

Your report in the Express of 6th May refers to the police once again promising improvements to the work they do and further reductions in the crime figures. I do hope that this time we see a reduction in the number of crimes committed and not just a reduction in the statistics.

I have been a critic of the police for many years and I am still of the opinion that if the Cheshire Constabulary was a business it would have gone into liquidation years ago due to gross inefficiency.

Having said that when the police do have a success they are not adequately supported by the judiciary. It is my opinion that some of our magistrates are totally out of touch with public opinion and reality. One can read in the paper every week of some of the ridiculous sentences handed out which do nothing to deter the offender or satisfy the public.

To take just one example from your paper. A driver caught speeding at sixty miles per hour in a forty mile per hour area, even though he had three previous convictions for speeding over the past three years, was not banned. It seems that the magistrates considered his job of more importance than the lives of the rest of us. His defence was that he did not see the sign. He has a Macclesfield address and according to the report was a regular driver in the area. Had I been the magistrate I would have imposed a ban of five years with a fine of £1,000 and ordered him to retake his driving test before renewing his licence.

I am of the opinion that a life ban should be automatic for anyone who causes death when driving over the alcohol limit. I also feel that all those banned should always have to retake their driving test. Unless magistrates hand out more appropriate sentences there is no incentive for the police to catch offenders. They are needed to boost the flagging morale of the local bobby, who, I am sure, feels under-valued and over-worked.

It is my opinion that the increase in crime is due to a large number of factors but amongst them are: the right of teachers to discipline their pupils, the removal of the parents right to chastise (not beat) their offspring, the citizens right to protect his own property from thieves or vandals, the stopping of national service without replacing it with some sort of service to the community, the education of those in their teens in the respect of others and the discipline of themselves, using social services as a prop and excuse for misbehaviour, government money to support and encourage single mothers, teenage pregnancy, and holidays abroad for persistent offenders as an alternative to punishment.

The police should adopt a zero tolerance policy on the laws that we do have. Stop the offenders at an early age before they become hardened criminals.

20TH MARCH 2002

Now is the time for a zero tolerance policy and for the police to be honest with the public. I, like many others, have frequently been the victim of crime and all I get is a letter saying that the crime is being investigated. That is in most cases not true.

If you are lucky enough to have a police officer attend the scene of a crime it is that officer who will decide if forensics should attend or if the crime merits further investigation. The outcome may depend on the mood of the officer or his current work load. If he feels there is little prospect of a conviction then the matter is just put on file until someone admits to the crime.

The criminals know that 60% of all reported crimes are not fully investigated and only 20% of reported crime leads to an arrest. It is like breaking the speed limit, we all do it because we know we will not get caught.

The biggest deterrent to crime is the fear of getting caught. I would gladly pay more for better policing but at present I would rather my council tax for the police went to the RSPCA. So Penny Wilson (Superintendent)*, bring back our police station from Wilmslow for a start, and put the police where they will do some good. I do not want to pay experienced officers for collating figures for the Home Office. We have had promises from your predecessors and so far none of them have made any noticeable difference.*

When I was a schoolboy I would have been afraid of getting caught by a policeman for an offence as trivial as stealing apples. I expect that we all have done that in our younger days but it was still theft. Most of us grew out of it and became sociably responsible. Some of today's kids have no respect whatsoever for the law and show no fear of arrest.

The youth of today are in the main good but those few who commit crime do not seem to know the damage they cause. They know that the law protects them more than it condemns them. Even the adults today seem to have an attitude of everyman for himself.

How many of us would tell a shopkeeper if we were given too much change? We are all a little dishonest so it is no wonder that children will live outside the rules of society. My views have not changed on this subject over the years.

DISHONESTY IS A NATIONAL HOBBY - 8TH JUNE 1989

If a census was taken, I expect that almost everyone interviewed would consider themselves to be law abiding citizens. The fact is, we all seem to break the laws daily and many of us consider the law is for other people. It is little wonder that crimes of all kinds are on the increase despite police figures. To my mind the figures only show fewer people report crimes as they believe the police to be impotent or unwilling to prevent many of the minor offences. Petty crimes often lead to greater crimes, in the younger generation particularly. Can we expect our children to obey the law when they see their elders ignore it daily. My observations lead me to believe that at least ten percent of all cars parked on the highway at night do so illegally in the sure knowledge that the police will take no action.

I notice that motorists ignore stop signs and treat red traffic lights with disdain. You can be sure each time the lights go red at least one car will go through. I have seen as many as five cars jump a single red light. How many motorists observe the speed limit? My experience is that when I travel at 30 mph everyone is trying to pass me. Can we believe that all those cars parking on pub car parks during opening times will all be driven away by orange juice drinkers?

It seems that almost everyone evades tax if they can, and claim excessively on insurance policies or defraud the DHSS to the detriment of the very poor and the honest; it's a national hobby.

But are we a happy nation? When did you last see a customer in Tescos or Sainsburys with a smile on their face? How many of you really know your next door neighbour? Are you free to walk in and out of his house as if it were your own? The chances are his doors are locked. It disturbs me that today emphasis is on protecting your property by locking, alarming and marking. We surely should be training our children in honesty, and deterring criminals by sensible punishments for their crimes. There are still countries in the world where people are honest and citizens respect the laws.

Perhaps our judges should be allowed the option of capital punishment. Why not consider castration for rapists. Perhaps the thought of cutting off the right hand for theft would make children think before theft and not consider crime as macho and probation as something to boast about.

We should all try to help each other and obey the unwritten law which suggests that everyone should be free to do as they please as long as that does not infringe on the freedom of others.

Parents, over the past twenty years, have stopped chastising their children. The teachers are no longer allowed to discipline their pupils. The policeman can no longer give a short sharp reprimand to a first offender. The magistrate is often totally out of touch with reality and a large band of do-gooders create a country of dependents. We must all shoulder part of the blame for the failure of our modern society to put good before evil and compassion before greed.

This article shows that nothing has changed in the last twenty years, the offences are still the same and the police still do not answer all the calls made to them. Today they seem to sit in their cars or are back at the station writing up their notes. There was a time when if you reported a crime a police officer would come out to your home and take a statement with a view to assisting you. If you have a fire the fire brigade will come to you, you do not need an appointment. If you have an accident a paramedic or an ambulance will come to you.

This change in procedure is new but the failure of a police officer to treat your problem as serious is not. I have been recording events now since 1970 and I will select just a few items to illustrate my point:

- Five children between the ages of 11 and 15 vandalised the caravans owned by the riding club. The police could not trace them so I did. Those concerned admitted their crime to school mates. The police took no action.

- An 18 year old was caught ripping panels off a building and the police identified him as a known villain but took no action as they thought it was a waste of police time.

- Six youths were caught damaging a sailing club house. The police took their names and addresses but took no further action.

- Seven youths were caught damaging the same building. The police were called but they never came.

- Three youths were caught breaking and entering a building. I called the police and held the culprits for two hours but the police never came so I had to release them.

- Five youths were caught trespassing and when ordered off the property one threatened me with a knife. I chased them off and when a WPC arrived with the kids still close by she said *"I'm not allowed to leave my car"*.

- 30th August 1983 my tractor was vandalised. I waited two hours for the police but they did not come.

- 19th April 1986 nine shots from an air weapon broke windows in a building but the police were not interested.

- 25th January 1987 caught three youths vandalising a building. One of the youths was caught and taken to court. Nearly success! It took six months to collect the ten pounds in damages ordered by the court. Following the case, just outside the court the father of the offender slapped him over the head saying *"that's for getting caught"*.

- 6th May 1987 caught a youth causing damage whilst trespassing on my land on a scramble bike. The police only charged him with not displaying a valid tax disc.

- 30th May 1987 five youths urinating in the street and throwing beer bottles. The police said there was no action they could take. It seems it was not an offence.

- The theft of a caravan, a tipping trailer, and a stone trough from my home - they attracted zero police interest. As a result I paid over £4,000 for new gates and CCTV.

- The CCTV has caught a number of offenders. All are clearly identifiable on the

The new wall at Holme Wood, Pott Shrigley, which the council told me that I could not lower without their permission. Everyone agreed it was an improvement when I had done the job.

The first sailing club building at Sutton Reservoir which was demolished after extensive damage.

The second sailing club building destroyed by teenage arsonists.

video. At the time of my writing, some four weeks after the police have got involved, they say they have got nowhere - but it took me only twenty minutes to get an identification on one of the youths. I wonder if the police want to catch the offenders - will it only create more work for them.

- In July 2000 travellers dumped five lorry loads of tree and other rubbish in my woodland. It seems that this is a civil matter and the police do not want to be involved even if we know who did it.

- 9th August 2001 three youths, at their third attempt, managed to destroy the sailing club at Sutton reservoir in an arson attack. The police eventually came, took one look, gave it a crime number presumably to cover any insurance claim, then left. No further action was taken despite the evidence at the scene.

- A pony of mine got out of its field. I reported the loss to the police. Some four weeks later I found the pony in a field two miles away. I approached the owner of the field and it appears that he reported finding the pony the same day as I reported it missing. The system cannot even cope with a lost and found horse.

- 1st December 1996 I found a lady's purse in my field thrown over from the main road. No money in it but photographs and a name and address. I reported the find to the police who told me that no one had reported the loss. I returned the purse to the owner on the 7th December. She told me that along with four others she had been robbed in Mill Street Macclesfield and spent four hours at the police station reporting the incident. She also told me that she rang on two occasion later only to be told her purse had not been found.

Even more worrying is the state of the 999 service. On the two occasions I did use it, when I had dogs worrying sheep, the police failed to respond. On one occasion they had the cheek to telephone me four hours later to ask if the dog was still there. It took me a couple of days to identify the owner and I gave the address to the police. They took no action so it was left to me to pursue the owner for the cost of a dead sheep.

I have on four occasions recorded instances of the police telling lies. One verbally, one by letter and most disturbing two whilst under oath in the crown court. I have also found a police cover up when I reported a driver jumping a red light on the Silk Road. Two very senior officers came to see me and told me that the vehicle was an unmarked police car on surveillance!

The Police Complaints Authority claim to be an independent body but I see them as a body to protect the police, much like the BMA protects doctors. If you make a complaint against an officer he is entitled to see a copy of that complaint - quite rightly so - but you are not entitled to see a copy of his defence. That seems odd.

I also believe officers will arrest a normally honest citizen with a fixed home address rather than chase a criminal. It is just easier. Recently I was arrested, handcuffed and held in a cell for several hours on the allegation of a female motorist that I had damaged her car. It took the police and the CPS months to decide that there was no case to answer and that no further action should be taken. Meanwhile my DNA was taken along with a photograph and my fingerprints, and put on file. Despite there being no evidence to justify a charge those records now cannot be removed.

The Police officer concerned had, in my opinion, a brain the size of a pea. He just decided to prove his manhood to his female assistant by arresting an OAP. I doubt if he is as brave when confronted with several aggressive teenagers. I made a complaint, currently under investigation by a senior police officer, and I was told that the police were wrong to arrest me and that I was entitled to a letter of apology from the chief constable. You too could well be arrested by an over-enthusiastic bobby who wants to increase his number of arrests to meet targets.

I think that what we really need is the return of the police house with a dedicated officer who knows his patch and the villains in his area. The degree of incompetence in the police force would not be tolerated in industry. The idea of targets is also something which prevents the police carrying out their duties.

I do not know if the police are any better or worse than they were in the 50s or 60s but they have a long way to go to regain the trust the public had then. I know that as a young man I had great respect for the police and put my trust in them, but now I would not trust a policeman. It is my verdict that we have far too many chiefs and not enough Indians.

David Bellamy opens the Middlewood Way.

Me in Army Cadet Force uniform at the age of fourteen whilst at King's school.

Prince Charles at the opening of the refurbished houses on Black Road.

The picture used on my election poster when I stood as an independent candidate for the Sutton and Langley ward.

FINAL THOUGHTS

I would just like to mention a few final things about my life.

I remember the visit to Macclesfield of Princess Elizabeth and her new husband on the 27th June 1949 when we were all marched from the school to take up a viewing point by the Central Railway Station. I still keep the medal presented to me by the school which commemorated the coronation of our new queen in 1953.

On the 8th February 1985 I met with Prince Charles when he came to open the refurbished houses on Black Road as the guest of Rod Hackney, the young architect. Rod was a great help to me when I was planning my house at Ecolodge and has remained a good friend ever since.

In 1990 I stood as an independent candidate for the council seat of Sutton as I always believed that you should not criticise others if you are not prepared to do the job yourself. I got 168 votes against the Conservative machine.

As a schoolboy my interests were trainspotting and birdwatching. Now I am a shareholder in Cheddleton Steam Railway and my nature study concentrates on trees and conservation - in my lifetime I know I have planted over twelve thousand trees.

My other hobby has been classic vehicles and in particular fire engines. As my job in the RAF was as a fire fighter it came naturally to restore a number of old fire engines. My favourite was a Thornicroft six wheeler which had seen service at Bristol Airport. It had a 18,500 cc Cummings diesel engine with a semi automatic gearbox.

It always turned heads at every show it went to. I still own a 1959 MK11 Ford Consul in sunburst yellow and in A1 condition - identical to the one I lost when I was young.

I was a founder member of the camera club along with Arthur Podmore and Peter Thornicroft, a member of the new Agricultural Society when Alderman Hidderley was in charge and Eric Oliver, the club secretary. I was one of the original members of the Prince Albert Angling Society along with Mr Newton and Arthur Smith.

I was treasurer of the Parkside Social Club, Scoutmaster of 9th Macclesfield (St John's) scout troop, one of the finest in the association, a member of the East Cheshire Combined Training Group and for six years a member of the committee.

I was President of the Macclesfield & District Riding Club and a founder member of the Macclesfield Riding for the Disabled group, for two years chairman.

I created the first self-sufficient house in England and two nature reserves. I always hoped that when I was gone I would be remembered for my contribution to self-sufficiency but I suspect that my legacy will be my two nature reserves.

I have written two books. *Macclesfield Demolished but not Forgotten* was very popular. The second was a tribute to my friend Les Cawley about the Anson Engine Museum, a project I was proud to be associated with. It was published recently.

On the 4th May 2002 I had a party at Oscar's in Chestergate, to celebrate my 65th birthday, when I invited a number of my closest friends and relations. It marked a milestone. I have had many ambitions and would like to have done more in my life. I feel that I have contributed in some small way to the success of the planet and not just taken from it. At the end of this little look into my life I am happy to feel that I have achieved as much, if not more than the average man.

When I have visitors to my home many of them remark on '*how lucky you are to live in such a beautiful place*' and I tell them that luck had nothing to do with it. All of it was achieved by vision, ambition, long-term planning and hard work. Not a bad way to plan your life - but you should also always try to do good, and treat your fellow man as you would have him treat you. I have tried to.